Papers Relating to Lord Eliot's Mission to Spain
in the Spring of 1835

Basque Politics Series No. 15

PAPERS
RELATING TO

LORD ELIOT'S MISSION TO SPAIN
IN THE SPRING OF 1835

LONDON 1871

WITH AN INTRODUCTION BY

XABIER IRUJO

Center for Basque Studies Press
University of Nevada, Reno
2020

PAPERS RELATING TO LORD ELIOT'S
MISSION TO SPAIN IN THE SPRING OF 1835

This work is the result of the collaboration of the Center for
Basque Studies with the Zumalakarregi Museum

Series: Basque Politics Series No. 15

Series editor: Xabier Irujo

ISBN-10: 1-949805-24-7

ISBN-13: 978-1-949805-24-6

Library of Congress Cataloging in Publication record data

Names: St. Germans, Edward Granville Eliot, Earl of, 1798-1877,
  author. | Gurwood, John, 1790-1845, author. | Wellington,
  Arthur Wellesley, Duke of, 1769-1852, author. | Irujo Ametzaga,
  Xabier, writer of introduction. | Irujo Ametzaga, Xabier, editor.

Title: Papers relating to Lord Eliot's mission to Spain in the spring
  of 1835 : London 1871 / Edward Eliot ; with an introduction by
  Xabier Irujo.

Description: Reno : Center for Basque Studies Press, University of
  Nevada, 2020. | Series: Basque politics series ; no. 15

Identifiers: LCCN 2020017572 | ISBN 9781949805246
  (paperback)

Subjects: LCSH: St. Germans, Edward Granville Eliot,
  Earl of, 1798-1877--Correspondence. | Gurwood,
  John, 1790-1845--Correspondence. | Wellington, Arthur
  Wellesley, Duke of, 1769-1852--Correspondence. | History-
  Carlist War, 1833-1840--Sources. | History--Carlist War,
  1833-1840--Foreign public opinion, British. | History--Carlist
  War, 1833-1840--Participation, British. | Prisoners of war.

Classification: LCC DP219.2 .S77 2020 | DDC 946/.072--dc23 LC
  record available at https://lccn.loc.gov/2020017572

Contents

Introduction	7
Papers Relating to Lord Eliot's Mission to Spain in the Spring of 1835	25
Instructions given to Lord Eliot by the Duke of Wellington	33
Despatches addressed by Lord Eliot to the Duke of Wellington	43
Private letters addressed by Lord Eliot to the Duke of Wellington	73
Private Letters addressed by Lord Eliot to Viscount Palmerston	79
Private Letter addressed by Lord Eliot to Mr. Villiers	83
Private Letter addressed by Mr. Villiers to Lord Eliot	95
Letters from Lord Palmerson to Lord Eliot . .	103
Letter from Lord Eliot to Mr. Backhouse . .	105
Convention	107
Diary of Colonel Gurdwood	111
Letters from Colonel Gurdwood	139
Appendix	179

Introduction

By the spring of 1835 the Basque Country was the seat of a brutal and cruel war. The Basques had been self-governed for over a millennium under their ancient laws. The kingdom of Navarra, created in 824 A.D. with the coronation of its first king, Eneko Aritza, had (in 1833) the authority to mint currency and had its own institutions, territory, customs and parliament. The same applied to the rest of the Basque states of Araba, Gipuzkoa and Bizkaia, which were governed as republics according to their laws and by their institutions. Fernando VII ruled in Spain and the Basque territories, respecting the administrative independence of all these states, but the outbreak of the French Revolution in 1789 and the Napoleonic Wars that followed (1803-1815) influenced the mindset of many Spaniards who, around the Liberal Party, pressed to create a constitutional and centralized Spanish state.

That was only possible through the abrogation of the Basque legal codes.

Unlike in the kingdom of Navarra and the rest of the Basque states, the Salic law ruled in the crown of Castile (Spain). Through the Salic law, cognatic male primogeniture was established, which excludes the females in favor of their sons in the succession of the throne. In 1829, Fernando VII's wife, Queen María Amalia, died without children. Due to the poor health of King Fernando, he designated his brother Carlos as heir. However, Fernando later married Queen María Cristina, who became his fourth wife. The marriage was celebrated on December 9, 1829 and on October 10 of the following year a girl, Maria Isabella, was born. The birth generated a conflict that would lead to the First Carlist War (1833-1839).

Queen María Cristina, close to the Liberal Party, defended the enthronement of her daughter, Isabella, for which it was necessary to repeal the Salic law. For his part, Carlos Borbón, Fernando's brother, demanded the recognition of his right to the throne and relied on the support of the majority of the Basque people who saw in him the guarantor of their particular codes of law and the maintenance of their private institutions against the Liberal Party. Their party became known as the Carlist Party and their followers, mostly Basques and Catalans, Carlists.

Fernando VII abrogated the Salic law not long before his death, and thereby transferred the right of succession from his brother Carlos to his daughter Isabella, who was still a child.

Fernando died on September 29, 1833 and on October 6 the first combats took place in the Basque mountains.

As Lord Eliot remarks, very soon the Queen Regent announced, by a proclamation, that those who took up arms for Carlos would be declared guilty of rebellion and thus treated as rebels. The Queen's officers accordingly shot every armed Carlist who fell into their hands. The Carlist army, which in the winter of 1833 consisted of eight hundred poorly-armed peasants and fourteen horses, by the spring of 1835 had become an efficient force of 28,000 men organized into thirty-nine battalions in control of much of the rural Basque Country under the command of General Tomas Zumalakarregi. Moreover, as Eliot reveals, every Basque peasant acted as a scout and brought him intelligence, which often enabled the general to surprise his adversaries and attack when they were unprepared for defense. He thus obtained, in the course of a few months, several victories. Battle by battle, Zumalakarregi beat the five generals that the Queen had sent to fight him, Luis Fernández de Córdoba, Vicente Quesada, José R. Rodil, Francisco Espoz y Mina and Gerónimo Valdés.

In light of the Queen's armies' policy of shooting Carlist prisoners as rebels, Zumalakarregi ordered the Queen's army prisoners to be shot as reprisal. However, as Charles F. Henningsen, Captain of the lancers in service of Zumalakarregi, wrote, in order to put an end to this dreadful state of things, he set free several soldiers who were in his custody. The Queen's army, however, continued the practice of putting prisoners to death in cold blood. In Eliot's opinion, this situation would have continued for months if no third party had intervened as a mediator between the belligerents. In 1835, the British Cabinet, headed by Sir Robert Peel, considered "the necessity of making some arrangement which should put an end to the mode of carrying on the war, which had excited the most painful sensations throughout Europe."

The Duke of Wellington became Secretary of State for Foreign Affairs in Peel's first cabinet (1834–1835) and in the spring of 1835 he entrusted Eliot with the mission to arrange for the exchange of prisoners and for the preservation of the lives of captive soldiers. The projected agreement for the treatment of prisoners contained nine ideas:

1. The Generals commanding the two armies engaged in operations had to agree that, in the case prisoners should be taken on either side, their lives shall be preserved.

2. No person whatsoever was to be put to death on account of the side he might be on, without previous trial, according to the laws or military ordinances.

3. Both the belligerent parties had to respect, and leave completely free, the sick and wounded found in hospitals, barracks, towns, farmhouses, or any other place.

4. It had to be agreed that exchanges of prisoners be periodical—once per week, or more often.

5. The exchange of prisoners had to be in exact proportion to the number of prisoners which each party shall present, and the number remaining over and above had to be retained by the party in whose power they were, until another opportunity of effecting an exchange should occur.

6. Officers were to be exchanged for officers of the same rank.

7. For their security and good treatment, prisoners had to remain with, and be guarded by, the party in whose power they were.

8. In case the war should extend to other provinces outside the Basque Country, the same arrangement was to be carried into execution.

9. The convention had to be strictly observed by the commanders-in-chief on both sides.

Wellington instructed Eliot that Carlos must not expect any change of circumstances regarding the relationships that the British, French and Portuguese administrations had with the Queen Regent's government. In sum, Eliot had to communicate to both parties that the British arbitration in relation to the exchange of prisoners did not involve, under any circumstance, support of the Carlist cause by the British government or any other European powers.

The British legation headed by Eliot arrived in Baiona on April 4, 1835. On April 13, Eliot requested from General Francisco Espoz y Mina, Commander of the Queen's troops in Navarra, safe conduct, to enable them to pass through the country occupied by the Queen's troops. Espoz y Mina complied with Eliot's request and offered protection and assistance on their journey.

When Eliot was in Baiona, Sir Robert Peel's Tory cabinet was dissolved and substituted by William Lamb's Whig administration. Considering that Eliot had been entrusted by the Duke of Wellington with his commission, he wrote to John Backhouse, Undersecretary for Foreign Affairs, to learn how to proceed. At this stage, Eliot assumed that he would probably fail at his mission, but he was determined to proceed, unless he received directions to the contrary from the new authorities in London.

On April 17, the legation passed into the southern Basque Country through the bridge of

Behobia and traveled safely to Irun, escorted by the troops of the Regent Queen. There, Eliot was received by the Governor and proceeded to Hernani with an escort of the regiment led by General Jauregi (called El Pastor or The Sheepherder). After having lunch in Hernani with Jauregi and his troops, Eliot kept on traveling. General Jauregi traveled in the carriage with Lt. Colonel Gurwood and Lord Eliot in the cabriolet with his staff-officer, Ignacio Empana. They arrived in Tolosa in the afternoon and the next day they were escorted to Lekunberri. The guides were alarmed by the presence of Carlist troops in the woods on the hill above the road, and stopped in Arribe. From there, the British legation continued to Lekunberri where the Carlist Junta, or Council, of Navarra was waiting to receive them.

In Lekunberri they dined with the Junta and the next day Colonel Antonio Serradilla led them through the corridor of Bi Haizpe to Irurtzun and Etxarri Aranatz. According to Eliot's description, the trip across the mountains from Tolosa to Irurtzun was fine and bold and the mountains were covered with snow. In Etxarri Aranatz the legation lodged for the night in the same place that the Duke of Wellington established his headquarters during the war against Napoleon in 1812. The village was destroyed and desolate due to the siege that had taken place on March 19, just one month earlier. General Zumalakarregi, aiming to put an end to the dreadful state of things, set free several soldiers who were in his custody and sent them to Pamplona under escort. Once the prisoners were set free, General Espoz y Mina ordered that the Carlist soldiers who had escorted the prisoners be thrown into prison.

On April 19, Eliot's legation went to Altsasu were two Carlist battalions under Generals Juan O'Donnel and Francisco Iturralde, second in command to Zumalakarregi, were waiting for them. From there, they proceeded through the country in which General Vicente Quesada had been defeated in April 1834 and, passing Zegama, they were escorted by General Juan Bautista Erro with about twenty lancers to Segura. The following day they met with Carlos. The pretender revealed that his officers had released many prisoners unconditionally, but that the Queen's generals had acted otherwise, shooting their prisoners. General Espoz y Mina, he added, had massacred all the sick and wounded found in the hospital at Escura [Ezkurra]. Carlos expressed his concern that his army, being constantly on the move, could not guard large bodies of prisoners. In addition, the Carlists were making many more prisoners than the Queen's troops, so that it would be very difficult to reach an agreement. Obviously, to release the prisoners on parole was not an option. Finally, Carlos added that any plan had to have the approval of his generals. After this short meeting, however, Eliot noticed Carlos' readiness to accept the principle of an exchange of prisoners.

From April 20 to 22, Eliot drew up the convention for the exchange of prisoners in Segura and gave it to Carlos and Cruz Mayor, Secretary of State of the Carlist government. Both Carlos and Cruz Mayor suggested several adjustments to the text, some of which were adopted and several declined as inadmissible and contrary to the instructions that Eliot had received from London. On April 22, the British legation learned that General Gerónimo Valdés had been appointed to command the Queen's forces in the Basque provinces and they started to receive reports of the battle that had taken place the two preceding days in the Amezkoa Valley between the forces of Generals Valdés and Zumalakarregi.

Later on, Eliot would be informed that Valdés, knowing that Zumalakarregi was fighting in the north of Navarra, had decided to attack what was considered the core of the Carlist territory, the Amezkoa. Valdés, with thirty-one battalions, had departed from Salvatierra on the 20th of April, and arrived at Kontrasta, in the beginning of the Amezkoa Valley. He entered the valley from Larragoa with a force of about 20,000 heading to Estella. On their way, the Queen's troops looted and burned several villages and took civilians as hostages. When his troops were half way to Estella, Zumalakarregi surprised Valdés with a small force. In the subsequent two-day battle, Valdés lost many of his men. The Carlists even plundered General Valdés' own baggage and tore the epaulettes off the shoulders of his officers. According to Lt. Colonel John Gurwood, Valdés' men numbered about twelve thousand, and that of Zumalakarregi around six thousand, 1,500 or less of whom were in action. The loss of Valdés was guessed to be about seven hundred men.

On the morning of April 24, Eliot received the corrected version of the convention from Cruz Mayor, and immediately proceeded to Olazagutia, and from there, to the Sierra of Andia through a beech forest. There Eliot could observe the tableland of Andia where the battle of the 21st and 22nd had taken place. From there they descended into the Amezkoa Valley and went to Eulate, at the bottom of it. However, Eliot was informed that Zumalakarregi had left in the morning for Asarta, twenty-five kilometers to the south. Finally, at 7:00 pm Eliot was received by Zumalakarregi at the door of his quarters in Asarta. After a short time, while Eliot was discussing the terms of the convention with Zumalakarregi and Carlos O'Donnel, Colonel Serradilla mentioned that ten of the Queen's soldiers, who had been brought in, had been ordered to be shot at daylight the following morning. Colonel Serradilla informed Lt. Colonel Gurwood that their lives could be spared at their intercession. Gurwood decided to mention the circumstances to Eliot, who immediately requested that Zumalakarregi spare the lives of the prisoners. Zumalakarregi granted Eliot's request at once.

Having been informed, the nine prisoners expressed their desire to thank Eliot. Zumalakarregi acceded, and the prisoners were brought up. As Eliot described, the sergeant threw himself on his knees, the others did the same, when Zumalakarregi told them to get up and thank Eliot for having spared their lives. They then expressed their gratitude to him, afterwhich Zumalakarregi said that he regretted that the British legation had not arrived the day before, as he would have spared the lives of the twenty-six prisoners shot on that occasion. Having heard that General Zumalakarregi had no spyglass, Lt. Colonel Gurwood requested from Eliot permission to give him his own, as a recognition of his act of clemency. This spyglass had been used by the Duke of Wellington at the Battle of Toulouse in 1814, and, Gurwood added, its value was now enhanced "by its being a memorial of his act of clemency towards the unfortunate prisoners."

Eliot and Gurwood were exceedingly well-received by Zumalakarregi and they had no difficulty in obtaining his signature to the convention. On April 24, Zumalakarregi sat for dinner with Eliot and Gurwood. Generals O'Donnel and Iturralde were also present. On the 25th of April, Zumalakarregi signed the convention. That day, Eliot and Gurwood met Charles Henningsen, who they described as "a fine handsome gentlemanly young Englishman, accomplished and speaking several languages, not nineteen years old, had been a volunteer and distinguished himself at Aranaz."

From Asarta the British legation went to Estella, hoping to find General Valdés in the city. They crossed the rich Berrueza Valley, covered in front by a ridge of hills from Monjardin towards Penacerrada. They passed through Piedramillera and reached the convent of Iratxe where the nuns welcomed them with chocolate and cookies. Zumalakarregi accompanied Eliot as far as within gunshot of Estella. When the garrison saw the Carlists approach, they were alarmed and began to fire while people everywhere cried "¡Viva Carlos V!" and showed great enthusiasm upon seeing General Zumalakarregi. Upon arrival at Estella, the legation was received with cries of "¡Viva la paz!, ¡Vivan los embajadores!, ¡Viva Dios!, and ¡Muera la puta!".

General Valdés was not present in Estella. Therefore, Eliot headed to Viana where that same evening he finally met with Generals Córdoba and Valdés. They suggested some corrections to the text and required some modifications. As a consequence, Lt. Colonel Gurwood returned to the headquarters of Asarta on April 26 to have General Zumalakarregi sign the amended convention. In the conversation that followed dinner on April 26, Eliot observed that Córdoba seemed to be an ostensible negotiator, while Valdés said very little and General Espartero seemed opposed to signing. The next day, April 27, Valdés signed the original as well as the amended copies of the convention in the headquarters of Logrono.

On April 28, Eliot and Gurwood went to Asarta over the mountains and snow, which led to some difficulties in preserving their tracks, and they had dinner with Zumalakarregi. They gave him the amended convention and read it to him, pointing out the suggested alterations. He answered that he did not want to quarrel about words and signed it. One day later, Eliot and Gurwood had breakfast with Generals Valdés, Espartero and Montenegro. They gave a list of prisoners to Valdés who promised to release them.

On April 30, they arrived in Viana where they once again met with General Valdés and departed with the column of six thousand troops and four cannons, commanded by General Aldama, to Sesma. One day later, the Duke of Wellington's birthday, they marched to Larraga in the rain, and continued to Mendigoria, Gares (Puente la Reina) under an incessant rain. They arrived soaked to the skin.

On May 2, Eliot and Gurwood went to Pamplona and lodged in the Casa de Redin. They had dinner once again with General Valdés and met Espoz y Mina and his brigadier, Vicente Sancho, who was much against the British intervention. Eliot and Gurwood did not like Espoz y Mina. Gurwood wrote in his diary that he had found him in bad health and that his inactivity and "the non-exercise of his military talents (if he ever had any more than those of a partisan), had done much injury to the Queen's cause during the last six months. His manner, an assumed mildness; but his conduct proved he was a wolf in sheep's clothing; against intervention, as are all his followers."

The next day they received a letter from Zumalakarregi requesting their intercession for a man and his wife confined in Pamplona, whose son had joined his army and died. That same afternoon Valdés released the man and the woman. On May 4, the legation headed back to Baiona through Atarrabia (Villava), Huarte and Zubiri, where they were taken before a Carlist post, in a gorge in the mountain. The officer in command was very civil and they proceeded with an escort, to prevent further detentions, to Auritz. There, they were received by a Carlist battalion. From Auritz they passed Luzaide (Valcarlos) and descended the Zize Port where the Battle of Rencesvals had taken place more than one thousand years before. They finally arrived in Donibane Garazi (S. Jean Pied de port) at 9:00 pm that night.

Eliot and Gurwood spent the morning of May 5 visiting the Citadel, "the Governor of which received us with much civility, but did not spare us a single bastion." After that, they saw what Gurwood described as a very extraordinary phenomenon, a cavity in the valley of eighty to one hundred yards in diameter, which was over one hundred feet deep. That night, they arrived in Baiona and had dinner with General Jean Harispe.

On May 6, they began a one-week trip to Paris passing through Toulouse, where they visited the battleground where Wellington had fought against Napoleon on April 10, 1814. On May 14, they arrived in Paris and met with Louis Philippe I at the Tuileries. He asked many questions relative to the necessity of French intervention for over an hour. While he personally was opposed to a French military intervention, he wanted to know whether it was desired and what might be the result of it. The King understood that France was a party to the quadruple alliance, but he and his ministers wanted to avoid armed intervention. Eliot and Gurwood expressed their opinion that without international intervention "there was not the most distant chance" of a termination of the war. Eliot was very explicit when he wrote that "I cannot but think that the war will continue and probably spread, unless the Queen's Government receive assistance from abroad. I have had this evening a conversation with General Valdés, in the course of which he made some statements of a remarkable nature. He described to me, in the first place, the state of demoralization in which he had found a great part of his army; and mentioned the facts, to which I have already referred, of his own baggage having been plundered by the troops on the night of the 22nd instant."

Having accomplished their mission, Eliot and Gurwood departed to London. Their work saved the lives of uncountable prisoners and helped humanize a long and cruel war that would not end until 1839.

The present book is a collection of papers related to Eliot's mission. The instructions that he received from the Duke of Wellington help elucidate the nature and purpose of his undertaking and Eliot's dispatches and letters give an account of what he accomplished. The journal of Colonel John Gurwood, who was fluent in Spanish and accompanied Eliot on his journey, and the letters addressed by him to Lord Fitzroy Somerset, add important information to this interesting story.

XABIER IRUJO

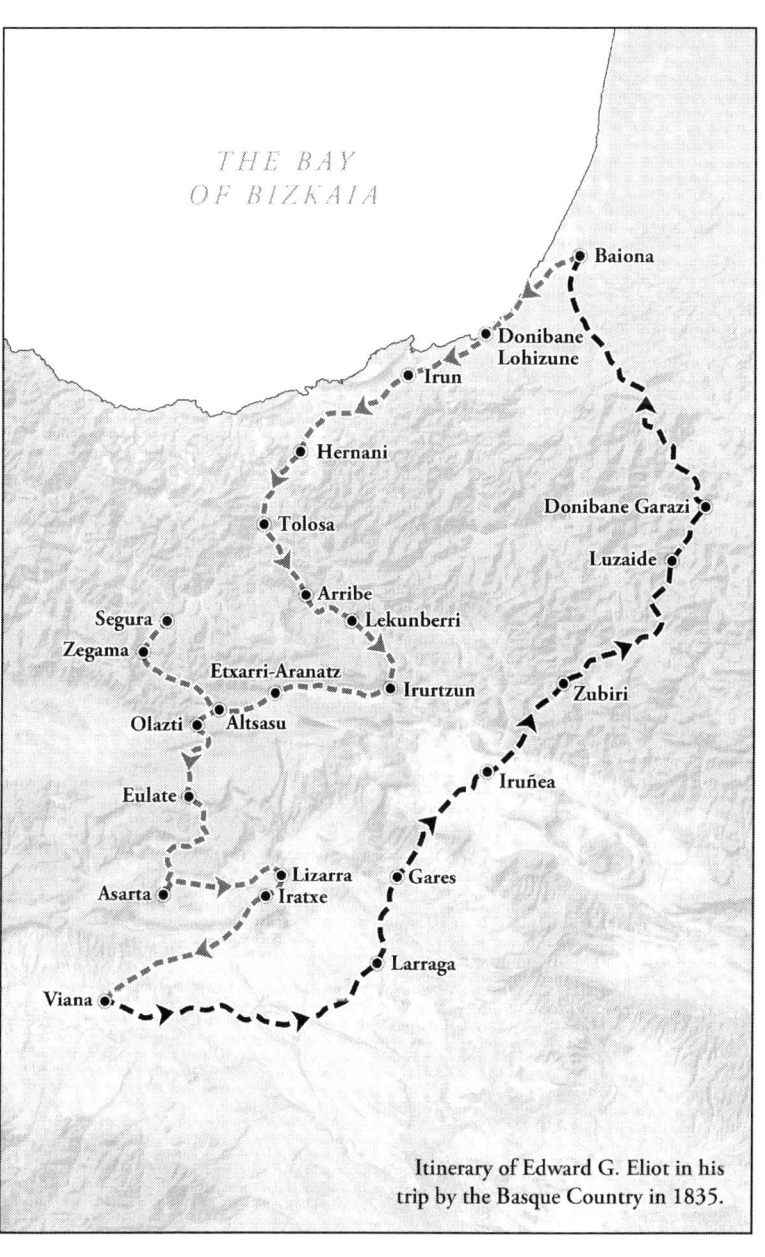

Itinerary of Edward G. Eliot in his trip by the Basque Country in 1835.

PAPERS
RELATING TO

LORD ELIOT'S MISSION TO SPAIN
IN THE SPRING OF 1835

ORIGINALLY PUBLISHED IN
LONDON IN 1871
BY
BICKERS & SON, LEICESTER SQUARE

In the Spring of 1835, the Duke of Wellington, who then held the office of Secretary of State for Foreign Affairs, entrusted me with a Mission to the Northern Provinces of Spain.

The following papers relate to that Mission.

The instructions which I received from the Duke of Wellington explain its nature and its objects: my dispatches and letters give an account of what I did in obedience to those instructions: the Journal of Colonel Gurwood,[1] who accompanied me, and the letters addressed by him to Lord Fitzroy Somerset,[2] contain a more minute record of all our proceedings.

In the Spring of 1835 the Northern Provinces of Spain were, and had for several months been, the seat of a sanguinary civil war.

This war arose out of the claim to the crown of Spain asserted by Don Carlos, after the death of his brother, Ferdinand the Seventh. Philip the Fifth had established in Spain the old law of France, commonly called the Salic Law, which restricted to males the right of succession to the crown. Ferdinand the Seventh, who had no son, abrogated this law, with the concurrence of the Cortes, not long before his death, and thereby transferred the right of succession from his next

---

[1] The Editor of the Duke of Wellington's Despatches, Colonel Gurwood, had served in the North of Spain, and the South of France, on the Staff of the Duke's army. Afterwards Lord Raglan; in 1835 Military Secretary to the Commander-in-Chief.

[2] Afterwards Lord Raglan; in 1835 Military Secretary to the Commander-in-Chief.

brother, Don Carlos, to his eldest daughter, the Infanta Maria Isabella, who was still a child. On the promulgation of a Decree to this effect, Don Carlos retired to Lisbon, and thence issued a protest against this act, as being an illegal one. Ferdinand the Seventh died in September, 1833, leaving a will, by which he constituted his wife, Queen Maria Christina, Regent of Spain for the period of her daughter's minority, and vested in her, in that capacity, all the powers of the crown.

The Cortes, the magistracy, and the army at once acknowledged Maria Isabella as Queen, and Maria Christina as Regent of Spain.

The people almost everywhere, except in the North, acquiesced in the assumption of power by the new Government; but in the North the inhabitants declared, almost unanimously, for Don Carlos, and many of them took up arms in support of his cause.

No sooner had the standard of Don Carlos been raised than the Queen Regent announced, by a proclamation, her determination to treat as rebels those who took up arms for him. The Queen's officers accordingly shot every armed Carlist who fell into their hands.

The Carlist chiefs were not slow to retaliate: they put to death, in like manner, every officer and every soldier of the Queen's army who became their prisoner. It thus came to pass that this war was carried on with greater barbarity than is usual even in civil wars.

Don Carlos remained at Lisbon till the beginning of June 1834. Early in that month he went on board an English ship of war, which was lying in the Tagus, and obtained a passage in her to England. His stay in England was very short. He crossed the Channel on the 1st of July, traversed France in disguise, and re-entered Spain on the 10th of the same month.

The Carlist army, which at first consisted of ill-armed, undisciplined, and almost independent bands, had by this time become an efficient force. It was still imperfectly armed and equipped; but it had been well-organized, disciplined, and drilled by Zumalacarregui, its able and energetic commander.

The presence of Don Carlos stimulated the zeal of the people in his cause, and strengthened their determination to make every sacrifice rather than abandon it: they accordingly redoubled their efforts to reinforce the army and to supply its wants. They succeeded so well in doing this that Zumalacarregui's troops were in a short time capable of coping with any force that the Queen's Government could send against them. Moreover, every peasant acted as a scout, and brought him intelligence, which often enabled him to surprise his adversaries and attack them when unprepared for defense. He thus obtained, in the course of a few months, several victories.

In the spring of 1835, the Queen's troops held all the fortresses in the Northern Provinces, and all the fortified posts, of which there was a chain along the high roads; but the Carlists were masters of every part of the country not in the vicinity of one of those strongholds.

The practice of putting prisoners to death in cold blood still continued, and would doubtless have continued during the war,[3] if no third party had intervened as a mediator between the belligerents.

The Queen's Government would not spontaneously have resolved to treat as prisoners of war men declared by it to be guilty of rebellion.

The Carlist chiefs would not have thought it possible to spare the lives of men who spared the life of no Carlist soldier.

The convention for the exchange of prisoners, which was framed by the Duke of Wellington, and which, after it had been slightly modified, was signed by the commanders of the two armies, proved to be effectual for its purpose. Not a single Spanish soldier was put to death in cold blood in the course of the four years which elapsed between the conclusion of the Convention and the end of the war.

Speaking in the House of Lords, on the 21st of April, 1837, the Duke of Wellington attributed

---

3   On the 31st of August, 1839, Maroto, who then commanded the Carlist army, concluded a Convention with General Espartero, who commanded that of the Queen, by which it was agreed that the Carlist troops should, on certain conditions, lay down their arms. This Convention terminated the war and extinguished the hopes of Don Carlos.

to me the success of the negotiation of which this Convention was the result.

All that I did in the matter was to carry his instructions into effect, as nearly as possible, and this the respect and deference felt for him by those to whom I conveyed his advice, made it easy for me to do.

I had, moreover, in conducting the negotiation, the valuable assistance of Colonel Gurwood, who spoke Spanish well, and was thoroughly conversant with the various military questions that we had to settle. A more useful or more agreeable coadjutor I could not have had.

I have had a few copies of these papers printed, in the belief that some of my friends will think that they are not, even now, wholly devoid of interest. To these papers I have appended two reports that I made in the autumn of 1823, to Sir William a Court,[4] of what passed at two interviews to which I was admitted by the Duke d'Angouleme,[5] who commanded the French army which was then besieging Cadiz.

St.Germans.

July 1, 1871.

---

4 Sir William a Court, afterwards Lord Heytesbury, was His Majesty's Minister in Spain. He had retired to Gibraltar when the Cortes compelled Ferdinand the Seventh to abdicate, and to accompany them to Cadiz.

5 His Royal Highness was a much more sensible and more moderate man than the world gave him credit for being. If he had possessed discretionary power he would, I am persuaded, have allowed Sir William a Court to act as mediator between the Cortes and the King, and have thus secured for Spain a Constitutional Government.

INSTRUCTIONS
GIVEN TO LORD ELIOT
BY THE
DUKE OF WELLINGTON

(No. 1.)

Foreign Office, March 26th, 1835.

My Lord,

Your Lordship is to proceed to Bayonne and endeavor to open a communication with His Royal Highness Don Carlos. You will inform His Royal Highness that you have a communication to make to him on the part of His Majesty.

If His Royal Highness should consent to receive your Lordship, you will inform His Royal Highness that the King had long observed, with concern, the manner in which the war was carried on in the Northern Provinces of Spain. That it was the practice in the armies of each of the belligerents to put to death the prisoners taken in battle.

That His Majesty, having lately received a report that certain Spanish Officers had been captured at sea in a ship sailing under British colours by a ship of war in the service of the Queen Regent, had applied to the Spanish Government, and had urged upon Her Majesty's consideration the necessity of making some arrangement which should put an end to the mode of carrying on the war, which had excited the most painful sensations throughout Europe.

Her Majesty had been pleased to give her consent to allow the King, in concert with the King of the French, to propose such an arrangement to His Royal Highness; and your Lordship will inform His Royal Highness, that you are deputed to attend His Royal Highness to confer with His Royal Highness upon the subject.

Enclosed your Lordship will find a Memorandum of an arrangement, which, if adopted in this simple form, and its terms strictly carried into execution, will attain all the objects in view.

I am, with great truth,
    My Lord,
        Your Lordship's
Most obedient, humble servant,

                WELLINGTON.

The Lord Eliot,
&c, &c, &c.

[Memorandum.]

(Enclosed in No. 1 to Lord Eliot.)

It shall be agreed between the Generals Commanding-in-Chief the two armies engaged in operations against each other in the provinces of Biscay, Guipuscoa, Alava, and Navarre, that, in case prisoners should be taken on either side, their lives shall be preserved, and they shall be exchanged upon the first occasion that will offer.

Exchanges of prisoners taken shall be periodical—once in each week, or oftener, if more frequent exchanges can be arranged. All prisoners taken on each side shall be given up on each occasion of an exchange; and an account of names and numbers shall be kept, so that the balance may be adjusted at the next period of an exchange.

Officers are to be exchanged for officers of the same rank.

No person whatever is to be put to death on account of the part which he may have taken, without previous trial and condemnation according to the laws or military ordinances.

In case the war should extend to other provinces, the same arrangement is to be carried into execution.

(No. 2.)

Tenour of observations to be made to Don Carlos.

Foreign Office, March 26th, 1835.

My Lord,

You will observe to His Royal Highness Don Carlos, that the form of a Memorandum to settle an arrangement for the exchange of prisoners has been adopted in preference to one more regular, in consequence of the earnest desire to attain the object, for the sake of all parties, without requiring from any the renunciation of titles, or the recognition of the titles or claims of others.

It is hoped that, considering the humane object in view, His Royal Highness will be disposed to adopt the course proposed to him.

I have the honour to be,
    My Lord,
        Your Lordship's
Most obedient, humble servant,

Wellington.

The Lord Eliot,
&c, &c, &c.

(No. 3.)

Further observations to be made to Don Carlos.

Foreign Office, March 26th, 1835.

My Lord,

It appears that there exists a decree of the Queen Regent of Spain, which directs that all officers taken in arms should be shot, and that all soldiers should be sent to the colonies.

If your Lordship should be informed that the issue of this decree was the cause of the retaliation on the part of the other party in the war, and its continued existence should be alleged to be the cause of the continuance of the existing practice, you will say that the execution of the decree must of course be suspended, by the signature of the Memorandum fixing the arrangement for the exchange of prisoners, and endeavours will be made at Madrid to have it recalled.

I am, with great truth,
    My Lord,
        Your Lordship's
Most obedient, humble servant,

                Wellington.

The Lord Eliot,
&c, &c, &c.

(No. 4)

To assure Don Carlos that England cannot recognize his claim to the Throne of Spain.

Foreign Office, March 26th, 1835.

My Lord,

It is desirable that your Lordship should avail yourself of an opportunity, while at the headquarters of His Royal Highness Don Carlos, to make His Royal Highness acquainted with his real situation and prospects.

England, France and Portugal are engaged by treaties of alliance with the Queen Regent of Spain. The object of these treaties is to prevent His Royal Highness from receiving by sea or by land any succours, whether in men, money, arms, or stores, or even a communication by letter or otherwise from any part of the world. It is impossible that this object should not be attained. His Royal Highness must not expect that any change of circumstances, whether in England or elsewhere, can alter the relations in which England, and France, and Portugal stand towards the Queen Regent; nor is it possible for any of the powers of the Continent, supposing any of them to be so inclined, to give His Royal Highness any assistance.

In truth, peace is the object of all the powers of Europe, and they would be unwilling to see it disturbed, for the purpose of attempting such an extensive system of war as must be carried on, in order to make the conquest of Spain, to promote His Royal Highness's possession of the throne of that kingdom.

On the other hand, His Royal Highness must be aware of the profound tranquillity which prevails in all parts of Spain, excepting those districts in which the existing warfare is carried on.

Your Lordship will inform His Royal Highness, that, although directed to state these circumstances to His Royal Highness, you have not been directed to make any proposition to His Royal Highness as resulting from them.

Your Lordship may inform His Royal Highness, that if he should think proper to withdraw from Spain, and to go to England, he will there have an asylum.

I am, with great truth,
    My Lord,
        Your Lordship's
Most obedient, humble servant,

                WELLINGTON.

The Lord Eliot,
&c, &c, &c.

(No. 5.)

Directions as to the course to be pursued by Lord Eliot after his interview with Don Carlos.

Foreign Office, March 26th, 1835.

My Lord,

In case Don Carlos should not consent to any arrangement for the exchange of prisoners of war, you will carry into execution your instruction No. 4, and return to England.

In case he should make any other proposition to the same effect, or should agree to the arrangement proposed in the Memorandum, you will dispatch Colonel Gurwood to General Mina's head-quarters and inform him thereof, and obtain his assent to any arrangement to which His Royal Highness Don Carlos may have assented.

General Mina will have been informed, and will have received his instructions from General Alava.

I am, with great truth,
    My Lord,
        Your Lordship's
Most obedient, humble servant,

                Wellington.

The Lord Eliot,
&c, &c, &c.

(No. 6.)

Foreign Office, March 21th, 1835.

My Lord,

I inclose to your Lordship a letter, together with its copy, which I have written to General Penne Ville Mur, with whom I am acquainted, and who I have learnt is at present at the head-quarters of the Infant Don Carlos, with the view of facilitating your Lordship's reception there.

Your Lordship will be able to judge on your arrival at Bayonne whether it will be most expedient for you to forward the letter from that city, or to deliver it personally to General Penne Ville Mur upon your arrival at the head-quarters of His Royal Highness.

I am, with great truth,

My Lord,
    Your Lordship's
        Most obedient, humble servant,
                Wellington.

The Lord Eliot,
&c, &c, &c.

[COPIE.]

Londres, le 27 Mars, 1835.

Mons. Le General,

Ayant appris que Votre Excellence se trou

Vait au Quartier General de S. A. R. l'Infant Don Carlos, je me rappelle a votre souvenir pour vous annoncer que Lord Eliot, qui aura l'honneur de vous envoyer cette lettre, est chargé d'une commission auprès de Son Altesse Royale par Sa Majesté Britannique.

Je prie Votre Excellence d'avoir la bonté de lui faciliter les moyens de s'approcher du Quartier Général, et de se présenter à Son Altesse Royale, afin qu'il puisse mettre en exécution la Commission dont il est chargé.

J'ai l'honneur d'être, M. le Général, avec la considération la plus distinguée, &c,

(Signé)

Wellington.

A M. le Général Penne Villemur.

Despatches addressed by Lord Eliot to the Duke of Wellington.

(No. 1.)

Arrival at Bayonne.

Bayonne, April 4th, 1835.

My Lord Duke,

I have the honour to inform your Grace that Colonel Gurwood and I reached Bayonne this morning.

I thought it right to make known to the French authorities as soon as I arrived my intention to open a communication with Don Carlos, and I have already received from them the strongest assurances of their desire to further my wishes in this matter.

The letter to the Count Penne Villemur with which your Grace furnished me, and one that I have addressed to that officer, will, I think, be delivered to him in about four days.

The head-quarters of Don Carlos are at Zuniga.

I have the honour to be, &c,

Eliot.

P.S.—I enclose a copy of my letter to M. Penne

Villemur.—E.

His Grace the Duke of Wellington, K.G.,
&c, &c, &c.

[Enclosure.]

Bayonne, ce 4 Avril, 1835.

M. Le Comte,

J'ai l'honneur d'envoyer ci-jointe à V. E. une lettre que M. le Duc de Wellington lui a adressée. Cette communication fera connaître à V. E. le but de mon voyage. Je me borne donc à lui annoncer mon arrivée à Bayonne, et à la prier de donner les ordres nécessaires pour que je puisse me rendre sans retard au Quartier Général de S. A. R. l'Infant Don Carlos.

Agréez, M. le Comte, l'assurance de ma considération le plus distinguée.

Eliot. S. E.

M. le Comte de Penne Villemur,
&c, &c, &c.

(No. 2.)

Safe Conduct, &c.

Bayonne, April 13th, 1835.

My Lord Duke,

I applied immediately after my arrival at this place to General Mina for a safe conduct, to enable me to pass through the country occupied by the Queen's troops.

General Mina has not only complied with my request, but has conveyed to several officers, commanding divisions of the army which he commands, strict injunctions to afford me protection and assistance.

In consequence of these injunctions I have received from Generals Oraa and Jauregui (the latter is commonly called El Pastor) assurances of their readiness to facilitate my progress, by giving me escorts, and by taking every other measure that may be thought necessary for that purpose.

I have, &c,

Eliot.

The Duke of Wellington, K.G.,
&c, &c, &c.

(No. 3.)

Reported resignation of General Mina.

Bayonne, April 15th, 1835.

My Lord Duke,

Mr. Harvey, His Majesty's Consul at this place, has received a letter from Colonel Wylde, dated Pampeluna, April 10, desiring him to inform me that there is reason to believe that General Mina sent to Madrid by the last courier his resignation of the command of the Queen's troops in the North of Spain.

Genl. Mina had not informed Col. Wylde of this fact; but as Col. Wylde seems to entertain no doubt of the accuracy of his information, I have thought it right to mention to your Grace what he has said.

Genl. Mina has been for some time past too ill to take an active part in the command of the army, and is said to have an incurable complaint.

I have, &c,

Eliot.

The Duke of Wellington, K.G.,
&c, &c, &c.

(No. 4.)

Has received Safe Conduct, &c.,from Head-Quarters of Don Carlos.

Bayonne, April 15th, 1835.

My Lord Duke,

The messenger, whom I despatched on my arrival at Bayonne to the head-quarters of Don Carlos, returned last night, bringing M. Penne Villemur's reply to my communication. M. Penne Villemur assures me that orders have been given

to the Commander-in-Chief of the army of Don Carlos to take every precaution to ensure my arrival at H.R.H.'s head-quarters.

It will thus be in my power to carry into effect your Grace's instructions so far at least as to make known to Don Carlos the anxious wish felt by H.M.'s Government that the barbarous practice of putting to death prisoners of war should be discontinued, and also to explain to H.R.H. the position in which he stands with relation to Foreign Powers. I purpose to leave Bayonne to-morrow, and hope to reach Don Carlos's head-quarters on the 18th or 19th inst.

I shall go by the way of Irun and Tolosa. Don Carlos was in the Borunda on the 9th, but he is now, I believe, in the Valley of the Amescoas.

The communication between that part of the country and the frontier is at present so insecure, that I may not have an opportunity of informing your Grace of the result of my mission before I re-enter France.

I have received great civility and attention from the authorities here.

I have, &c,

Eliot.

The Duke of Wellington, K.G.,
&c., &c., &c.

(No. 5.)

Arrival at Tolosa, &c.

Tolosa, April 17th, 1835.

My Lord Duke,

I left Bayonne yesterday evening, accompanied by Colonel Gurwood, and reached Tolosa this afternoon.

On crossing the Bidassoa we found a detachment belonging to the division of General Jauregui under arms and ready to escort us. At Oyarzun we found that officer himself, and were accompanied thence by him to this place, which is his usual head-quarters. Bodies of troops were stationed along the road at short intervals, and furnished us successively with escorts.

The country through which we passed appears to have suffered little from the war. I have learned since my arrival here that the head-quarters of Don Carlos are now at Onate, a town near Bergara, but as I have reason to think that an officer of H.R.H.'s staff will be in readiness at Lecumberi to conduct us, I intend to proceed in the first instance to that place.

I have, &c,

ELIOT.

The Duke of Wellington, K.G.,
&c, &c, &c.

(No. 6.)

Arrival at Segura.

Segura, April 20th, 1835.

MY LORD DUKE,

Don Carlos is now at this place,—a small town between Tolosa and Salvatierra.

I arrived last night, conducted from Lecumberi by an officer of the Infanta's staff, and I had an audience of H.R.H. this morning.

The conveyance by which I send this despatch is too insecure to allow of my stating in it the particulars of our conversation.

I have, &c,

Eliot.

The Duke of Wellington, K.G.,
&c, &c, &c.

(No. 7.)

Conversations with Don Carlos and with M. Cruz Mayor.

Segura, April 20th, 1835.

My Lord Duke,

On being admitted this morning into the presence of Don Carlos, I asked H.R.H. to permit me to read to him a Memorandum which I had drawn up, containing the substance of the instructions given to me by your Grace on the subject of the proposed agreement for the exchange of prisoners.

When I had read it Don Carlos said that he had no difficulty in admitting the principle which it sought to establish, that he had for a long-time refused to sanction the practice of putting prisoners of war to death, and that he had not consented to do so till the General commanding the Queen's troops had promulgated a decree of the Government at Madrid awarding the punishment of death to all persons taken in arms against that Government.

He went on to say that he had since released many prisoners unconditionally, but that his example had not been followed by the Queen's Generals. On the last occasion, the taking of Echarri-Aranaz, the soldiers whom he sent to escort the prisoners to Pampeluna had been seized, and were still confined in that fortress. General Mina, he added, had massacred all the sick and wounded whom he found in the hospital at Escura.

I observed that the proposed agreement would at once put a stop to such proceedings. To this he assented; and promised to consider my proposition as it deserved. He expressed however an apprehension that the difficulty of framing a practicable measure will be very great.

I next read to H.R.H. another Memorandum which I had prepared, explaining the position in which he stands with regard to Foreign Powers.

This Memorandum, of which I enclose a copy, is little more than a translation of the Paper marked No. 4, which forms part of my instructions.

Of the stipulations of the Treaty, therein referred to, Don Carlos said that he was quite aware. "Had a system of neutrality and non-intervention been acted on by Foreign Powers, I should now," he exclaimed, "be on the Throne of Spain. The people are with me. Nothing but their enthusiasm could keep me where I am. The Queen is supplied with arms, with stores, and with money from abroad. I have no resource, but the zeal and devotion of the Spanish people."

To this I only replied that I had been instructed to make this communication to H.R.H., but not to submit any proposition arising out of it to him.

I then retired accompanied by M. Cruz Mayor, the titular Secretary of State for Foreign Affairs, who had been present at the interview. M. Cruz Mayor, as soon as we were alone, entered into conversation, by saying that I might rely on Don Carlos's disposition to agree to an exchange of prisoners, but that I could not expect him to be a party to an arrangement of which his opponents would derive all the benefit.

The Carlists, he continued, possess no fortified places, and are constantly moving about. How then can they guard large bodies of prisoners? To release them on parole would only be to send them back to serve in the Queen's army. Moreover they make many more prisoners than are made by the Queen's troops, so that it would be impossible to strike a balance.

Any plan that might be devised must, he added, be sent to the Generals for their advice and opinion. Don Carlos could do nothing in the matter without consulting them.

M. Cruz Mayor then expressed some fear that the acquiescence of Don Carlos in a proposition of this nature might be looked on by the Queen's Generals as an indication of weakness and of inability to retaliate. The proposition ought, he said, to be first agreed to by the party with which the practice in question originated.

I answered, that Don Carlos's admission of the principle would be of little avail if he were determined to reject the only means of giving effect to that principle: that no plan which could be framed would be free from all objection; but that if both parties were in earnest, every real difficulty might, I was persuaded, be easily obviated. I accordingly suggested that he should send me back my Memorandum, with such modifications of the plan proposed in it as Don Carlos might, after consulting his Generals, deem essential.

I should willingly, I assured him, modify the proposition according to the wishes of Don Carlos before I submitted it to the Queen's Generals, provided that the alterations desired by him appeared to me to be reasonable and consistent with the attainment of the object in view.

With regard to the dread felt by M. Cruz Mayor, that the acquiescence of Don Carlos in a proposition not yet acquiesced in by the Queen's Generals would be looked on by them as an indication of weakness and of inability to retaliate, I remarked that neither party, in accepting the offer made by the King my master to mediate between them, and in agreeing to terms proposed by him, could be said to make an overture to the other.

I remarked further, that, as H.R.H.'s clemency even now induced him to release many prisoners, the agreement would be more advantageous to his troops than to those of the Queen.

To this he replied that the releasing of prisoners was now an act of generosity, which it would cease to be when made a matter of agreement.

M. Cruz Mayor then adverted to the second Memorandum which I had read to Don Carlos, and told me that he trusted that I did not require an official answer to that communication. It would, he said, be difficult for him to do so without using stronger language than might be deemed proper by the King's Government.

As an individual in Don Carlos's confidence, he could assure me that nothing would make H.R.H. abandon the cause in which he was engaged, and that he was prepared to defend to the last extremity his own rights and those of the Spanish people.

I told M. Cruz Mayor that the communication in question deserved the serious consideration of

H.R.H. and of his advisers, but that it required no formal answer.

I do not think it necessary to repeat more of the conversation which I had on this occasion with M. Cruz Mayor.

Before we separated he promised to send me back without delay my Memorandum, with the proposed modifications of the plan contained in it.

I have since received from him the note of which I enclose a copy.

I have, &c,

ELIOT.

His Grace the Duke of Wellington, K.G.,
&c, &c, &c.

[ENCLOSURE No. 1]

Segura, ce 20 Avril, 1835.

La guerre civile qui désole les Provinces Septentrionales de l'Espagne occupe depuis son commencement l'attention du Roi mon Maître.

Il voit avec douleur l'esprit de vengeance qui anime les deux partis, et qui a fait naître l'usage atroce de mettre à mort les prisonniers de guerre.

La prise d'un bâtiment marchand Anglais, ayant sur son bord plusieurs offIciers Espagnols, par un bâtiment de la Marine Royale Espagnole, a fourni au Roi une occasion convenable de faire des représentations à cet égard à la Reine Régente.

La Reine Régente, écoutant les conseils du Roi vient d'autoriser le Général, qui commande son armée, à signer une convention pour l'échange des prisonniers.

Le Roi est persuadé que l'Infant Don Carlos n'hesitera point à donner la même autorisation au Général qui est à la tête de ses troupes, et il m'a ordonné de conférer avec S. A. R. sur les moyens d'effectuer cet accord.

Le projet de convention que j'ai l'honneur de soumettre à S. A. R. est rédigé, de la manière la plus simple, mais il n'en sera pas moins efficace si les conditions en sont strictement remplies. Il n'exige des parties contractantes aucune cession de droits, aucune renonciation de titres, il n'a pour but que d'arrêter l'effusion de sang.

Dans le cas ou S. A. R. consentirait à autoriser le Général qui commande ses troupes à signer ce projet de convention, tel qu'il est, ou avec des modifications qui n'en détruiraient point l'effet, je me rendrais auprès du Général en Chef de l'armée de la Reine, et je l'engagerais à y mettre son nom.

De plus, le Roi mon Maître fera tous ses efforts pour procurer la revocation du décret de la Reine Régente qui prononce la peine de mort contre tout officier au service de S. A. R. Don Carlos, et contre tout soldat celle de la déportation.

Eliot.

[Enclosure No. 2.]

[memorandum.]

Je suis chargé d'éclairer S. A. R. sur sa véritable position. Je dois lui représenter que par le Traité du 22 Avril, 1834, avec ses Articles additionels du 18 Août de la même année, la France, le Portugal, et l'Angleterre sont tenus d'empêcher que S. A. R. ne reçoive, de quelque parti que ce soit, aucun secours, soit en troupes, soit en argent, soit en armes, soit en munitions de guerre. S. A. R. ne doit point s'attendre à ce qu'un changement de circonstances quelconque qui peut survenir en Angleterre, ou ailleurs, pourra rompre les engagemens qu'ont contractés les gouvernemens d'Angleterre, de France, et de Portugal, envers la Reine Régente.

Quant aux autres Puissances Européennes, elles ne sauraient non plus seconder les vues de S. A. R. La paix c'est l'objet des vœux de toutes les Puissances, et elles ne voudront point troubler la tranquillité générale pour entreprendre de placer S. A. R. sur le trône d'Espagne.

Mes instructions, en me prescrivant le dévoir de faire cette communication à S. A. R. ne m'autorisent point à lui soumettre des propositions, basées sur les circonstances qui en font le sujet. Si toutefois S. A. R. se decidait à quitter ce royaume, je suis à même de l›assurer qu›elle trouvera un asyle en Angleterre.

(Signé)

Eliot.

Segura,
  ce 20 Avril, 1835.

[Enclosure No. 3.]

Readiness of Don Carlos to admit the principle of an Exchange of Prisoners.

[Translation of note from M. Cruz Mayor.]

Royal Head-quarters of Segura, 29 April, 1835. The King Don Carlos V., my august master, in consequence of the communication which your Lordship, in the name of His Britannic Majesty, made to him this morning at the audience which H.M. granted to your Lordship, has commanded me to inform your Lordship that very far from H.M. being disinclined to give to Europe authentic evidence of the humane principles by which his heart has ever been animated, no one (in his opinion) will be able to deny the acts, public and notorious, by which, since his arrival in his kingdom, H.M. has manifested his clemency and generosity; and this two-at-a-time when as yet no foreign power had thought of urging its own particular opinions with regard to the system of warfare adopted in this country.

The barbarous conduct of the enemies of H.M. in respect to the treatment of prisoners was the sole motive which impelled the Generals of Carlos V., after having borne with it for a long time, to have recourse to reprisals; not however, as persons are apt to suppose, out of a spirit of revenge, but rather with the view of checking by this means the excesses of our adversaries, and forcing them to enter within the regular limits of civilised warfare.

The treatment of prisoners taken in the actions of the 27th and 28th of October—those of Los Arcos, and of Echarri-Aranaz—and various other occasions of the same nature, clearly attest a predisposition on the part of H.M. to be merciful towards his enemies.

The burning of Lecaroz, and the butchery of its unoffending inhabitants, besides many previous acts which it would be grievous to enumerate, afford melancholy proof of the inhumanity which has been met with on our side from the partisans of the Queen.

I need not, on this occasion, refer to the disorders and the assassinations perpetrated by an unbridled populace in the chief towns of the provinces, and even up to the threshold of the Court itself, since the very journals in the pay of the opposite party have caused them to be sufficiently notorious.

There is no right-minded and impartial person but must be convinced of the truth of what I state, and whose inward judgment will not lean in favour of Carlos V., my Sovereign.

It is therefore superfluous to assure your Lordship of the readiness with which H.M. will entertain any propositions tending to assure the kind treatment of prisoners, and to rescue them from the miserable fate which awaits them in the system of warfare now actually in force.

Nevertheless, since this barbarous law was originally the work of our enemies, it is indispensably necessary that they should be the first to revoke it; and it is essentially just, moreover, that, as the result of the desired Regulation, the balance of disadvantage should not fall to the deserving troops of H.M., and that the greater benefit should not accrue to their adversaries.

If a Regulation should be proposed setting forth in writing terms of perfect equality between the two belligerent parties, H.M. will agree to it with pleasure.

This, my Lord, is the answer which H.M. dictates to me, and I hasten to make it known to your Lordship, availing myself of the opportunity to offer to your Lordship the assurance of my high consideration.

CARLOS CRUZ MAYOR.

The Lord Eliot,
    Envoy of H. B. M.

(No. 8.)

Appointment of General Valdes to the Command of the Queen's Troops.

Segura, April 22nd, 1835.

MY LORD DUKE,

General Valdés has been appointed to the command of the Queen's forces in the north of Spain. No convention between the contending parties will therefore be valid without His Excellency's sanction.

I shall consequently take on myself to submit to General Valdés the terms of the convention to which Don Carlos is willing to accede.

In communicating under these circumstances with General Valdés and not with General Mina, I am, I conceive, adhering to the spirit of my instructions though I depart from their letter.

General Mina continues to hold the office of Viceroy of Navarre, but the functions of it are, I believe, purely civil.

I have, &c,

ELIOT.

The Duke of Wellington, K.G.,
   &c, &c, &c.

(No. 9.)

Has received Don Carlos's modification of the proposed arrangement for the Exchange of Prisoners.

Segura, April 23rd, 1835.

MY LORD DUKE,

I have just received from M. Cruz Mayor a paper containing the arrangement for an exchange of prisoners as modified by Don Carlos.

Your Grace will perceive on looking at the translation of it, which I enclose, that it contains two conditions which do not exist in your Grace's Memorandum.

The first of these provides that some one or more villages or towns shall be declared neutral, and that either party may detain their prisoners therein without molestation by the enemy until an exchange can be effected. This provision is considered to be indispensable by the advisers of Don Carlos, as without it they would not have the means of securing their prisoners. Conceiving that strong objections will be made to it by the Queen's Generals, I endeavored to prevail on M. Cruz Mayor not to insist on its insertion. The council however, to whom this matter was submitted, were inflexible on the point, and I thought it better to endeavor to obtain the assent of General Valdés to the arrangement as it now stands, than to break off the negotiation.

The other article merely stipulates that the sick and wounded in hospitals shall be respected. I can anticipate no objection to this, and had no hesitation in admitting it.

A scheme so impracticable and absurd was originally devised by M. Cruz Mayor, that it is hardly worthwhile to give an outline of it. He proposed that the prisoners should by conveyed to England in ships to be provided by His Majesty for that purpose; and that they should be detained there until they could be exchanged. The expenses attendant on this arrangement to be defrayed by the party in Spain which should in the end be victorious.

I have, &c,

ELIOT.

The Duke of Wellington, K.G.,
    &c, &c, &c.

(No. 10.)

Completion of the Arrangement for the Exchange of Prisoners.

Logroño, April 29th, 1835.

My Lord Duke,

I took my departure from Segura on the 24th instant, and on the following day reached Asarta, a village in the mountains, about three leagues from Estella. At this place I found General Zumalacarregui, and was exceedingly well received by him. I had no difficulty in obtaining his signature to the convention of which I was the bearer.

The lives of ten prisoners who were brought in while I was at Asarta, and who were about to be shot, were at my request spared by General Zumalacarregui.

From Asarta I proceeded to Estella, hoping to find General Valdés at that place; it was not, however, till I reached Viana that I came up with His Excellency. He then told me that he was about to continue his march to Logrono, and that he wished to postpone all discussion of the subject which I came to propose for his consideration until the next day.

The same evening, however, soon after my arrival at this place, I had the honour of a visit from Generals Valdés and Cordova. General

Valdés, in the course of the conversation which took place on this occasion, showed the greatest desire to further the object in view, but pointed out several articles in the convention which appeared to him not to be clearly expressed, and to require some modification. He, however, assured me that he was ready to sign the convention as it was, accompanying it with a paper explanatory of the sense in which he understood the articles in question, rather than put an end to the arrangement. Before we separated he undertook the following day to place in my hands a statement of the objections which he felt to the convention as it stood, and of the alterations which he wished to be made.

The next morning I received from General Valdés a note, of which I enclose to your Grace a translation. I also enclose a copy of my reply. It appeared to me that the simplest and most satisfactory mode of arranging this matter was to prevail on General Zumalacarregui to allow the convention as amended by General Valdés to be substituted for that which he had already signed. I therefore requested Colonel Gurwood to proceed to Asarta and to explain to General Zumalacarregui that the alterations appeared to me to be only verbal, and not to affect the principle of the arrangement. In the event of General Zumalacarregui declining to accede to the proposal of signing the amended copy, Colonel Gurwood was to deliver to him the original convention executed by General

Valdés, placing at the same time in his hands a declaration drawn up by General Valdés of the sense in which he understood some of the articles.

Colonel Gurwood returned last night from Asarta, bringing with him the amended convention signed by General Zumalacarregui. Colonel Gurwood was accompanied by General Montenegro, who is authorized by General Zumalacarregui to settle the details of the arrangement with an officer to be empowered for the same purpose by General Valdés.

I transmit to your Grace, Colonel Gurwood's account of his interview with General Zumalacarregui. It is with great satisfaction that I announce to your Grace the successful termination of this affair, and the completion of an arrangement which there is reason to hope will be the means of saving many lives, and of checking the spirit of vengeance which now actuates both parties in these provinces.

My anticipations that difficulties would be made by General Valdés to the recognition of the neutrality of one or more towns have not been realized, and I think it due to His Excellency to state that he has behaved on this occasion with the most perfect frankness, and with a real desire to bring to a prompt and satisfactory conclusion the business which I have had to conduct.

I have the honour to be,
>   With the greatest respect,
>   My Lord Duke,
>   Your Grace's
Most obedient, humble servant,

> > > > ELIOT.

The Duke of Wellington, K.G.,
>   &c, &c, &c.

[SEPARATE.]

State of affairs in the Northern Provinces.—
Conversation with Generals Valdés and Cordova.

> > Logroño, April 22nd, 1835.

MY LORD DUKE,

I think that it is my duty to lay before your Grace the result of the observations that I have made, and of the information that I have received, respecting the state of affairs in the parts of Spain through which I have passed.

I have now traversed the theatre of war in almost every direction. I have seen both the contending armies, and I have conversed with persons of every class and of both parties. My opinion, founded upon what I have thus seen and heard, is distinctly that the resources of the Queen's Government are wholly insufficient to enable them to bring the war in the Northern Provinces to a successful termination.

A great part of the country in which hostilities are carried on is almost inaccessible, except to the lightly armed and lightly clad mountaineers, who compose the army of Don Carlos.

I believe Don Carlos to have at present about 12,000 or 14,000 men formed into battalions, besides numerous bands of armed peasants, who intercept the communications and cut off the convoys of the Queen's troops.

The peasants, being almost without exception Carlists, bring constant and accurate information of the movements of the Queen's troops, and prevent Her Majesty's Generals from obtaining any knowledge of the operations of the Carlist army.

The Carlist army is abundantly supplied with provisions, whilst that of the Queen can scarcely procure the necessary rations. Food of every kind is cheap in the country, while in the towns it bears a comparatively high price.

Events which have recently occurred appear to me to make that certain which I before thought probable.

The Government has lately made great exertions in order to equip an army sufficiently strong to restore order in the Northern Provinces. Of this army General Valdés put himself at the head, and in order to signalize his assumption of the command, he lost no time in bringing his troops into conflict with those of Zumalacarregui. The engagement took place on the 22nd instant, in the mountains bordering on the Valley of the Amescoas. Different accounts are given by the two parties of this affair; but there can be no doubt that the result was unfavourable to the Queen's troops. The effect has been to demoralize them to a great degree. As a proof of this, I am enabled to assure you that they plundered the luggage of the Commander-in-Chief, and tore the epaulettes from the shoulders of some of their own officers on the night that the enemy entered Estella.

General Valdés has retired to this place, and is endeavouring to re-organize his army, but in the meantime the Carlists increase in numbers and become more daring, and it will require a far larger force than any which can now be brought by the Government against Zumalacarregui to conquer, or even to cope with him.

What would be the effect of the entrance of a French force? This is a question on which I feel the greatest diffidence in hazarding an opinion. I think it right to tell your Grace, that great repugnance to foreign and particularly to French intervention has been expressed to me by several officers of rank in the Queen's army. Some few of them would, I am inclined to believe, actually join the Carlists, whilst many others would resign their commissions. The army at large would certainly view with jealousy the arrival of French troops, and it would require a force overwhelming in point of numbers to bear down the resistance which the Carlist troops would continue to offer, formed, as they would be, into guerilla bands. The term of occupation must moreover be indefinite, as the retreat of the French would be the signal for the recommencement of the present state of things.

The expense too would be enormous.

On the other hand, I cannot but think that the war will continue and probably spread, unless the Queen's Government receive assistance from abroad. I have no means of judging of the general feeling of the inhabitants of the Provinces to the South of the Ebro; and I cannot, therefore, say what prospect there is that Don Carlos will be enabled to carry the war further in that direction; but of the Provinces in which hostilities now take place, he has entire possession with the exception of the fortified towns, and of the ground actually occupied by the Queen's troops.

I have had this evening a conversation with General Valdés, in the course of which he made some statements of a remarkable nature. He described to me, in the first place, the state of demoralization in which he had found a great part of his army; and mentioned the facts, to which I have already referred, of his own baggage having been plundered by the troops on the night of the 22nd instant, and of several of the officers having been stripped of their epaulettes by their own men. He went on to say that, in the late action, the troops generally had shown much backwardness, and that the officers in particular had betrayed a want of spirit. While talking on this subject, General Valdés seemed much depressed. He next adverted to the extreme violence of the ultra-liberal party in Spain, and said that the Government was placed in a situation of great embarrassment, for that while it was employing all its energies to quell the Carlist Insurrection, the Republican party were creating disturbances which it required vigilance and force to repress. He then mentioned that he had, within the last two days, received applications for troops from the Commanders-in-Chief in Castile and in Catalonia, and from the Governor of Santander. With these applications it was impossible for him to comply, unless he were to do so by weakening his own army, which was already insufficient for its purpose.

General Valdés proceeded to say, that he had always been averse to foreign intervention, and that he still considered it as a measure pregnant with danger to the independence of Spain; but that the existence of the social state in the country was now at stake: that a dissolution of all Government was now to be apprehended, and that he confessed he now looked to foreign aid as the only means of avoiding anarchy.

General Valdés expressed a strong wish that a small English force could be sent to occupy some points in Spain, whenever the advance of a French army should be determined upon. Such a manifestation of H.M.'s feeling in favour of the Queen's Government would produce, he said, a very strong moral effect. General Valdés mentioned Bilbao and St. Sebastian as the points which he wished to be occupied by British troops.

General Cordova holds precisely the same language as to the necessity of intervention, and goes even further in declaring the hopelessness of the present attempt to restore order in the Northern Provinces. He is likewise, if possible, more desponding than General Valdés in his view of the general state of affairs in Spain.

I believe that I have repeated the substance of what was said to me by Generals Valdés and Cordova, and I do not think it necessary to trouble your Grace with any observations upon their statements.

I have, &c,

ELIOT.

His Grace the Duke of Wellington,
&c, &c, &c.

Private Letters Addressed By Lord Eliot To The Duke Of Wellington.

Conversation with M. de Broglie.
Paris, March 30th, 1835.

My Dear Duke,

I think it right to inform your Grace, that I waited on the Duke de Broglie this evening by His Excellency's desire.

He told me that he wished much that my departure could be delayed for a few days, as the French Government would now be placed by it in a situation of great embarrassment; that they had been led to expect, by a despatch from M. de Rayneval, that the Duke de Frias would by this time have been furnished with instructions formally to request the King of the French to unite with His Majesty in proposing an arrangement to Don Carlos; but that so far from this being the case, the Duke de Frias had that morning, in a conversation with him (M. de Broglie), declared that he had received no such instructions, and that although the Queen of Spain would view with pleasure the adoption of any measures tending to stop the effusion of the blood of her subjects, yet that she could not consent to take any step inconsistent with the dignity and independence of her Crown.

M. de Broglie added, that the impression produced on his mind by the Duke de Frias's language was, that the Queen's Government is more than indifferent to the proposed measure.

He concluded by expressing an earnest hope, that the Spanish Cabinet would take the initiative in this matter: that he was most desirous that the efforts of France should be united on this occasion with those of England; but that it was impossible for the King, his Master, to send a commissioner to Don Carlos unless invited to do so by the Queen. Should the requisite application be made in the course of a few days, as he hoped it might, he would, he said, send orders to General Harispe, who commands on the Frontier, to direct an officer of rank to accompany me from Bayonne to Don Carlos's head-quarters.

The Duke de Broglie then expressed the pleasure which it gave him, to think that the fallacious expectations so long entertained by the Carlist party, would be destroyed by your Grace's communication to Don Carlos.

I have, &c,

Eliot.

His Grace the Duke of Wellington, K.G.,
    &c, &c, &c.

(No. 2.)

State of affairs in the Basque Provinces.

Bayonne, April 6th, 1835.

My Dear Duke,

I have endeavored to make some use of my time here, and to gain an insight into the state of things on the other side of the Frontier. With this view, I have conversed with persons of different opinions, and have tried, by comparing their statements, to form an idea of the truth.

Writing by the post, I do not like to mention names; but I may say that the persons, to whom I refer, are in a position which entitles their statements to attention.

Your Grace will, I am sure, pardon me for telling you, plainly and without reserve, what impression has been made on my mind by the various communications that I have received.

That impression is, that the Queen's Government is unable to put down the Insurrection in the Basque Provinces; and that the Carlist cause is daily gaining ground in that part of Spain.

I will mention a few facts, at least what I believe to be facts.

Zumalacarregui has altogether from 18,000 to 20,000 men, most of them good soldiers, and with some exceptions well-armed and equipped:

provisions are abundant (bread and meat little dearer than in ordinary times), and money is not wanting.

Zumalacarregui is, as your Grace knows, an active and enterprising leader, and his men are full of enthusiasm. The mass of the people is, moreover, unquestionably with him.

The Queen's troops, on the other hand, show but little zeal. Of the recruits, which leave Castile and the other Provinces for the North, a large proportion desert on the road.

I have said that Zumalacarregui is abundantly supplied in every respect. Whence are his supplies drawn? There can be little doubt, from France. Stores of all sorts pass the Frontier every day; and the authorities take little pains to prevent them passing. Vigilance, I have reason to believe, is not very strongly recommended to them by their superiors. I can only speculate on this part of the question, and it is, perhaps, presumptuous in me to trouble your Grace with speculations; but I will not conceal from your Grace my belief, that the French Government either think that they have an interest in the continuance of the present state of things, or wish that things may be brought to such a pass as to compel the Queen's Government to apply to them for assistance.

Of one thing I am convinced, and that is, that the entrance of a foreign force is essential to the restoration of the Queen's authority in the North of Spain.

Few or no supplies are introduced by sea, and our blockade is a matter of little importance as long as an unlimited quantity can be brought in by the French frontier.

I have seen but few Carlists, and have derived my information principally from well wishers to the cause of the Queen.

I have thought it right to make known to your Grace my opinion, and the grounds on which it rests; but I trust that nothing which I have said will lead you to suppose that I shall deviate a hair's breadth from the course prescribed by my instructions.

I have the honour to be, &c,

ELIOT.

His Grace the Duke of Wellington, K.G.,
    &c, &c, &c.

Return to Bayonne.

Bayonne, May 6, 1835.

My Lord,

I have the honour to inform your Lordship that I reached. Bayonne last night on my return to England.

It is from Mr. Harvey, H.M.'s Consul at this place, that I have learnt the fact of your Lordship's appointment to the office of Secretary of State for Foreign Affairs, a despatch which was addressed to me by your Lordship and forwarded from hence by Mr. Harvey not having reached me. From Logrono, which place I quitted on the 30th ult., I proceeded in company with General Valdés, and reached Pampeluna on the 2nd inst. At Pampeluna I remained a day for the purpose of paying my respects to General Mina, and on the 4th I resumed my journey to this place.

It is my intention to set out to-morrow for England.

I have, &c,

Eliot.

The Viscount Palmerston,
    &c, &c., &c.

Private Letters Addressed By Lord Eliot to Viscount Palmerston

[SEPARATE.]

Conversation with M. San Miguel, &c.

Further Observations on the State of Affairs in the Northern Provinces of Spain.

Bayonne, May 6th, 1835.

My Lord,

I had several opportunities, whilst on the march from Logrono to Pampeluna, of conversing with several of the superior officers of the army of General Valdés. I talked amongst others with Don Evaristo San Miguel, who was Secretary of State for Foreign Affairs in the years 1822 and 1823. It is difficult to describe the repugnance which M. San Miguel expresses to foreign, and especially to French, intervention. It was better, he said, that Spain should suffer all the horrors and all the calamities of a protracted civil war, than that she should be indebted for deliverance from them to the aid of foreigners. In the first place, he thought that the occupation of the disturbed provinces must be of indefinite duration; for that the temporary presence of foreign troops would at the best afford only a temporary respite from the existing evils; and in the next place, he said, that if Spain was not herself capable of defending her institutions, she was not worthy of enjoying them.

I pressed him to explain what measures he thought it would be advisable that the Government should take under existing circumstances. He replied in vague terms: «II faut faire un appel au patriotisme de la nation,» «II faut sortir de l'orniere oil nous sommes,» were some of the phrases which he used. All that I could collect was that he thought that the present Government did not enjoy the confidence of the people, and could not consequently command the exertion of all their energies, and that the formation of a more liberal ministry and the adoption of a more liberal policy were necessary measures. M. San Miguel did not scruple to say that the resources at the disposal of General Valdés were inadequate; and acknowledged that as yet no progress had been made towards the re-establishing of the Queen's authority in the Northern Provinces.

General Lopez, who commands the cavalry, and several other officers of rank, seem to dislike as much as M. San Miguel the thought that application is likely to be made for foreign intervention, and they declared their readiness to make any sacrifice rather than submit to the humiliation which such a step would bring on the Spanish army.

General Mina, whom I saw at Pampeluna, appeared to be sanguine as to the result of the present campaign; but said that should General Valdés be unsuccessful, he saw no reason to despair, and he expressed a hope that under no circumstances would the Government sue for foreign assistance.

General Mina is ill; but he did not appear to me to be in a dying state.

The weather was very bad during the march to Pampeluna, and the troops suffered a good deal from its effects.

The defeat of General Iriarte, in Biscay, the news of which reached this place yesterday, will, I cannot but think, produce a very unfavorable effect in the Basque Provinces. The situation of those inhabitants of the towns who are well affected to the Queen's Government, is pitiable. I was assured by a respectable man, in whose house I lodged at Puente de la Reyna, that he had not ventured out of the town for fourteen months; and that his family was obliged to sleep every night in the fort. There is a population in Puente de la Reyna of 5000 or 6000 souls, and thirty-six persons only have enrolled themselves in the Urban guard. This, I believe, to be a fair instance of the state of most of the towns in the Basque Provinces and Navarre.

I am impressed with a strong conviction, that under the circumstances of the case, General Valdés will find himself compelled to desist from offensive operations, and will probably soon retire beyond the Ebro.

I have the honour, &c,

Eliot.

The Viscount Palmerston, &c, &c, &c.

Private Letters Addressed By Lord Eliot to Mr. Villiers.

(No. 1.)

Conversations with M. de Broglie and M. de Frias.

(Copy sent in private letter to the Duke of Wellington, of the same date.)

Paris, March 31st, 1835.

My Dear Villiers,

Before this letter reaches Madrid you will have been informed of my appointment as Commissioner to Don Carlos, and will have received a copy of my Instructions. I will, therefore, only tell you what has taken place since my arrival at Paris. I first saw Lord Cowley, and was not a little surprised to hear that the French Government is not only unprepared to send a Commissioner to act in concert with me, but is desirous that I should delay my departure.

I afterwards saw the Duke de Broglie, and was informed by him of the reasons which induce the French Government thus to halt, as it were, in their march.

They had been led by M. de Rayneval to expect that the Duke de Frias would by this time have received instructions to request the King of the French to join His Britannic Majesty in proposing an arrangement to Don Carlos. M. de Broglie said that he had seen M. de Frias that morning, and had been assured by him that he had received no instructions to that effect. M. de Broglie added, that the impression made on his mind by M. de Frias's language was, that the Spanish Government was by no means desirous that the King of the French should make any proposition to Don Carlos. I do not recollect the exact expression quoted by M. de Broglie, but its purport was, that although the Queen of Spain would rejoice at the prospect of being enabled to put a stop to the effusion of blood, yet that she could consent to no measure which would be derogatory to the dignity of her Crown. It was impossible, M. de Broglie went on to say, for the King, his master, to make any proposition to Don Carlos, or even to communicate with him, until he had been formally requested by the Queen of Spain to do so.

He was, however, he assured me, fully sensible of the importance of an apparent, as well as of a real, concert and union in this matter between the Cabinets of France and of England; and it was for this reason that he wished me to postpone my journey, till it had been ascertained whether the Queen of Spain would or would not make the requisite application to the French Government.

I replied that I was not at liberty to delay my departure, but that I must necessarily remain some days at Bayonne.

He then said that he was so desirous that the French Government should take part in the proceeding, that if the application were made in time, he would send an order by telegraph to General Harispe to commission a French officer of rank to accompany me to the head-quarters of Don Carlos.

This morning I had a conversation with the Duke de Frias, and his Secretary of Embassy, M. d'Ayllon.

They evidently consider the appointment of a French Commissioner to be neither necessary nor desirable, and think that the Cabinet at Madrid take the same view of the question.

M. de Frias is instructed to act in concert on every point (procediendo en todo de acuerdo) with General Alava, but he does not construe that to mean that he is to call on the French Government to send a Commissioner to Don Carlos, because the English Government sends one with General Alava's consent.

He thinks it of the utmost consequence that the communication from the English Government, of which I am the bearer, should be made to Don Carlos; but he does not think that a similar communication from the French Government would produce any important results. He apprehends that the opponents of the Ministry in the Cortes might represent the mission of a French agent to the head-quarters of Don Carlos as an act of intervention, but would take no exception to the presence there of an English Commissioner.

No mention was made, he said, in his Instructions, of this application to the French Government, and he was not prepared to incur the responsibility of acting without instructions in so serious a matter.

I observed that he was desired to act in concert with General Alava, and that he would act according to the spirit of his instructions by doing at Paris what General Alava had done in London. To this he replied that General Alava had only approved of the appointment of an English Commissioner, and had not solicited it.

I did not think it necessary to say more on the subject, so our conversation stopped here.

I leave Paris this evening, and shall probably reach Bayonne on Sunday. I shall apply to Don Carlos, as soon as I arrive there, for a safe-conduct to his head-quarters. I shall also request the Generals commanding the various divisions of the Queen's army to furnish me with passports.

I shall not receive these papers for some days, so that the French Government will have sufficient time to consider whether I am or am not to proceed alone.

Always,
My dear Villiers,
Very truly yours,
ELIOT.

(No. 2.)

Offers to be the Bearer of any Proposition that the Queen's Government may wish to make to Don Carlos.

Bayonne, April 4th, 1835.

MY DEAR VILLIERS,

I had no safe means of forwarding the accompanying letter from Paris, and therefore brought it on to this place. As I am anxious to receive an answer to this letter before I proceed to Don Carlos's head-quarters, and find that the ordinary post is very long on the road, I send my pacquet by a courier.

You know the limits of my commission, and are aware that, as H.M.'s Commissioner, I can make no proposition and hold out no expectation to Don Carlos with a view to induce him to withdraw his pretensions; but I cannot help thinking that my presence at his head-quarters is a circumstance of which the Government of the Queen of Spain might, nay ought, to take advantage.

Putting out of the question all considerations of humanity, and looking only to the pounds, shillings, and pence, they must wish to end the present state of things. Let them make Don Carlos a bridge of gold, and he may be tempted to cross it. I am aware that there are great difficulties in the way of such an arrangement as I suggest. I know that the Cortes have declared Don Carlos a traitor, and that any negotiations with him would excite a great deal of clamor; but I know also that the object in view is an important one. I desire then to be informed whether the Queen's Government will make any, and if any, what, terms with Don Carlos and his followers; and, if so, whether they will authorize me to signify to him their disposition to treat.

In offering to become the channel of communication, I have no desire to put myself forward. It would, I conceive, be very difficult for the two parties to open a negotiation between themselves; but it would be less so to carry it on if matters were put in train for them, and to put matters in train is all that I propose to do.

Any advice or suggestions that you can give me will be most gratefully received.

I have written in such haste, that I am afraid that I have hardly made myself intelligible.

    Yours ever,
        Very truly,

                Eliot.

(No. 3.)

*Conversations with Don Carlos
and M. Cruz Mayor, &c.*

Paris, May 14th, 1835.

MY DEAR VILLIERS,

Your letter of the 1st was brought to me yesterday, a few hours after my arrival here. I regret very much that, in writing to you, I did not enter more at large into the details of my proceedings in Spain, since the meagerness of my communications seems to have occasioned some disappointment, both to you and to the Spanish Minister.

It would be of no use now to make excuses for my omission. I will, therefore, proceed at once to make the best reparation I can by telling you what took place. I must, however, just observe that I had very few opportunities of writing; that I had a good deal to do, and that I thought that in telling you that I had negotiated a convention, I implied that I had done nothing else.

The fact is, that my instructions only authorized me to communicate to Don Carlos the views of our Government, and to put an end to any expectations that he might have formed of obtaining assistance from Foreign Powers. To suppose that such a communication would induce Don Carlos to retire from the contest, would be rather an unreasonable supposition.

No promise, no quid pro quo, on the one hand; no threat on the other. To go to Don Carlos and to say to him, "Sir, you had better withdraw," would be to draw forth the same sort of observation that your ancestor, the witty and extravagant Duke of Buckingham made, when Sir John Cutler advised His Grace, who was complaining of poverty, to live as he did. "Live like you, Sir John," said the Duke, "why, I can do that when I have not a shilling left." Don Carlos can retire when he has neither men nor money. He will always have that pis aller.

When I arrived at Segura, I thought that the best way of opening my communication with Don Carlos was to read my instructions to him. I accordingly drew up two Memorandums, one relating exclusively to the proposed cartel; the other, to the views and intentions of the English Government. I need not repeat what passed between us respecting the former. On my reading the latter to him, he said that he was aware of the engagement into which the King had entered, when he signed the Treaty of the Quadruple Alliance, and that he neither expected nor hoped more, than that the English Government would allow the feeling of the Spanish people to show itself.

He went on to say, that if a system of neutrality and non-intervention had been acted on, he should by that time have been at Madrid. The mass of the people, he declared, were with him. It was their enthusiasm alone which kept him where he was. The Queen received supplies of money, of arms, of ammunition, and of stores from abroad. He had no resources, save those which he found in the zeal and devotion of his followers.

I did not think it necessary to controvert these assertions, and contented myself with observing that I had been instructed to make this communication, but not to submit any proposition to him.

H.R.H. ended the conversation by saying that he had hoped that the Duke of Wellington would have taken a course less unfavorable to him.

I afterwards saw M. Cruz Mayor, his faiseur, a sharp little man, but rather tricky.

After discussing the question of the cartel, and pointing out various difficulties in the way of the proposed measure, he proceeded to speak of the second Memorandum, and said that he hoped that it was unnecessary for him to make, on the part of the King, his master, any formal reply to it. Were he to do so, he could not help making use of stronger language than might be deemed consistent with the respect due to H.B.M.

As an individual, enjoying the confidence of Don Carlos, he could assure me that nothing would induce him to abandon the enterprise in which he was engaged.

I merely said, in reply, that the communication which I had been instructed to make to H.R.H.

deserved his serious consideration; but that it did not require an answer. I gave M. Cruz Mayor a copy of this Memorandum, in order that he might make himself fully acquainted with its scope.

I subsequently, on more than one occasion, recurred to this subject, but he appeared to be determined not to enter again into a discussion of it.

I may observe, that, as M. Cruz Mayor understands English, I read to him the original Paper, No. 4, of my instructions.

I have now repeated the substance of what passed with reference to the Duke of Wellington's communication, and I have only to add that I do not, at present, see any chance of its producing the desired effect. You say, that I appear to think French intervention necessary.

What I meant to say is, that the means at the disposal of the Commander-in-Chief of the Queen's troops are, in my opinion, insufficient to enable him to put an end to the war. Spain may, for aught I know, possess the resources requisite for that purpose; and if she have not, it may, perhaps, be a less evil to allow the war to continue than to call in French troops to occupy the Northern Provinces for an indefinite period.

I have already stated my opinion respecting the state of public feeling in the Basque Provinces and in Navarre. Even in the towns, the lower classes are Carlists. At Puente de la Reyna, with a population of from 5000 to 6000, there are but thirty-six urbanos; and the bourgeois, in whose house we lodged, told me that he had not ventured to go outside the walls of the town for fourteen months. On the approach of a body of Carlists, he dreads a rising of the populace, and sends his family for safety to the casa fuerte.

Zumalacarregui has now at least 10,000 men formed into battalions, besides a considerable number of aduaneros and armed peasants, who intercept the communications and cut off convoys.

In the affair of the Amescoas, Valdés lost about 400 men. His rear-guard was very roughly handled, and his troops generally were so thoroughly demoralized, that they plundered the General's own baggage and tore the epaulettes off the shoulders of their own officers.

Look at the map, and you will be puzzled to account for Valdés's movements. From Vittoria to Salvatierra, thence to Estella by the Amescoas; from Estella to Logrono, from Logrono to Pampeluna.

Cordova accuses Valdés, without reserve, of incapacity. He is going to Madrid, and will no doubt repeat to you what he said to me on the subject.

Valdés did not scruple to acknowledge that he was much disappointed at the result of his first operations. He complained of the state of his army.

I concluded that he held the same language in his communications to the Government, and that you would learn from them what he thinks of the state of things. The King of the French is strongly opposed to intervention. M. de Broglie told the Duke de Frias that if the new Ministry in England desired that a French Commissioner should be sent, it would be necessary to submit the question for consideration to the Council. This is not the ground which he took when I was here, on my way to Spain. France is afraid now of giving umbrage to the Northern Powers.

I am to see the King, and the D. de Broglie, this evening; but as I leave Paris to-night, I shall probably not write to you again, unless I have something very interesting to communicate.

> Ever,
> Yours very truly,
> ELIOT.

Private letters addressed by Mr. Villiers to Lord Eliot.

(NO. I.)

Spanish Government cannot treat with Don Carlos.

Madrid, April 15th, 1835.

My Dear Eliot,

I received yesterday your letter of the 5th inst., and have communicated it to the Spanish Government. As I expected, they consider it impossible to make any offer to Don Carlos or his partizans, and I must add in their justification that it would be as much as their lives are worth to do so. The solemn acts passed by them, without opposition, in both Estamentos, against Don Carlos, and the excited state of public opinion upon the whole subject, would render a compromise of any kind with the insurgents fatal to the Government, if not to the Queen's cause. Much as I feel the truth of what you say upon the desirableness of such a measure upon grounds of humanity, policy, and economy, I would not, were I a Spanish minister, act otherwise than they do—i.e., as to originating any proposition—if one were made to them they might, perhaps would, take it into consideration, but I fear that nothing which Don Carlos would propose would be accepted by the Government; for they would have to go to the Cortes for a sanction which they assuredly would not get. The only thing you could with safety to yourself do, in the event of Don Carlos wishing to treat, would be to forward his proposals to me, to be submitted to the Government, without pledging yourself as to their adoption or rejection.

Your mission excites the greatest interest here, and hopes are founded upon it which I fear have little chance of realization. Don Carlos, I believe, desires to quit the country, but he is entirely under the savage control of Zumalacarregui, to whom his presence is useful in the concoction of the barefaced lies by which his party is kept together and encouraged. I have not the least doubt that he will publish to the insurgents that you are the English Ambassador come to recognise Don Carlos, and, when you leave the headquarters, that you are gone home to fetch assistance—in short, these are the kind of means resorted to. I think therefore it would do no harm if you let it percer at Bayonne that England never would recognise Don Carlos, and intends to take every means for putting an end to the war. I wish with all my heart that I had any advice to give you, it should be at your service in your most difficult task of bringing so many wolves to acts of kindness and brotherly love. This letter too will only reach you when you have probably done or not done your business, and advice or opinions would come too late. My only regret is not having directed Colonel Wylde, who is at the head-quarters of the army, to go and meet you at Bayonne; he is a sensible, observing man, and might have smoothed your difficulties, and you would still do well to send for him (should you be in want of any such assistance), upon my authority, as he is attached to this mission during his stay in Spain.

I am sprawling upon the sofa with a fit of the gout, so you must excuse this illegible scrawl. Pray let me hear from you again. I wish you all success, my dear Eliot, in your negociations, which I am sure could not be in abler hands. The difficulties may perhaps be insurmountable, but, if not, you will be the greatest benefactor this country has known for many a long year.

Yours ever truly,

GEORGE VILLIERS.

The Lord Eliot,
  &c, &c, &c.

(No. 2.)

Spanish Ministers pleased with the result of Lord Eliot's Mission, but not prepared for his opinion that French intervention was necessary to put down the Carlists.

Madrid, May 2nd, 1835.

My Dear Eliot,

I have received your letter from Logrono, of the 27th ult., and one of the 28th, from Wylde, in which he seems to suppose that you have given me a full account of your mission to Don Carlos. Perhaps you wrote on the 28th, as well as Wylde, but I have not received the letter, and in that of the 27th you only mention that Don Carlos was taken aback by your instructions, and that some slight alterations were made in the Cartel. I have not, therefore, been able to tell the Spanish Government whether your mission is likely to have political results, for which, of course, they care more than the humane objects you had in view. However, they are much pleased with what you have brought about upon that matter, though I should have liked to know whether Valdés has reported everything correctly, and in default of information from you, I am not able to correct his version. Martinez de la Rosa and Toreno are greatly inclined to defer to your opinion, and when I told them you thought French intervention necessary, they were as much taken aback as Don Carlos would be; but I would not tell them the precise grounds upon which your opinion had been formed. I wish, with all my heart, that the report of your being about to come here, which I saw in a Pampeluna paper, were true. It would have been a great service to the Government, who have nearly as many lies told them from- the theatre of war as Don Carlos. I should, of course, have written to you before, but there were no means of sending letters, and I now only write this for the chance of its meeting you on your way home. You have had a perilous, but I should think not an uninteresting tournee, and have, I am sure, performed as much as was possible, and more than I expected. We have all been rather deceived respecting the feeling of the population; there appears more enthusiasm and less exhaustion than I believed to exist. The change of Government in England will, in my opinion, make French intervention much more difficult than before. The Duke of Wellington, if he had consented to it, might easily have induced the Holy Alliance to take the same views as himself. Melbourne's Government will not be able to do so, and Louis Phillippe will think twice before he enters Spain to support a juste-milieu system (the only one which can save Spain), with all the Powers of Europe remonstrating against it. The whole subject makes a pleasant puchero.

Kent House, September 16th, 1838.

My Dear Eliot,

I have returned your box of papers to Ward, but I cannot leave London without thanking you for having allowed me to read them, and repeating what I have always expressed in every quarter, my admiration of the manner in which you conducted and successfully concluded your difficult negotiation—of it's beneficent results, nobody has been in a more favourable position than myself for judging, and I am sure it will always be a satisfaction to you to reflect, that hundreds upon hundreds of families bless your name in Spain, and that you have been the means of sparing misery and bloodshed to an incalculable amount. I say you advisedly, for although the merit of projecting the convention is of course due to the Duke of Wellington, yet if the negotiation of it had been confided to hands less skilful, or to a person who would have permitted party feelings to interfere with the object to be attained, the scheme would inevitably have failed, and the war would then have become even yet more horrible from the increased exasperation of the belligerents.

I return to that unfortunate country to-morrow, and not with a very light heart, for it will only be to witness what one must deplore and cannot prevent or mitigate. Believe me always, my dear Eliot,

Very truly yours,

George Villiers.

Eliot.

> Yours always,
>> My dear Eliot,
>>> Very truly,
>>>> GEORGE VILLIERS.

I send this to Paris, though I have not the remotest guess when it will reach you.

Letters From Lord Palmerston To Lord Eliot.

(No. 1.)

Announcing Appointment as Secretary of State for Foreign Affairs.

Foreign Office, April 17th, 1835.

My Lord,

I have the honour to acquaint your Lordship, that the King has been pleased to accept of His Grace the Duke of Wellington's resignation of the office of His Majesty's Principal Secretary of State for Foreign Affairs, and to confide to me the Seals of that department. I am accordingly to desire that you will in future address to me your despatches and letters on public business to be laid before the King; and you will receive from me such orders and instructions as His Majesty shall think proper to give for your guidance and direction.

I am, with great truth and regard,
    My Lord,
        Your Lordship's
    Most obedient, humble servant,

            Palmerston.

The Lord Eliot,
  &c, &c, &c.

(No. 2.)

Foreign Office, May 22nd, 1835.

My Lord,

I have the honour to acknowledge the receipt of your Lordship's despatches to No. 12 inclusive, which have been laid before the King.

I have received His Majesty's commands to signify to your Lordship His Majesty's entire satisfaction at the manner in which you have executed the mission committed to your charge at the seat of hostilities in the Northern Provinces of Spain.

The success which has attended the execution of your instructions for the interchange of the prisoners taken in battle, and the consequent introduction of a more humane system of warfare between the contending parties, is a source of sincere gratification to His Majesty and His Government.

I have the honour to be,
    My Lord,
        Your Lordship's
    Most obedient, humble servant,

            Palmerston.

The Lord Eliot,
  &c, &c, &c.

Letter from Lord Eliot to Mr. Backhouse.

Reasons for proceeding, notwithstanding the resignation of Sir Robert Peel's Government.

Bayonne, April 12th, 1835.

My Dear Sir,

The intelligence which has this moment reached me, of the dissolution of Sir Robert Peel's Government, makes me desirous of troubling you with a few lines.

Entrusted by the Duke of Wellington with a delicate commission, I am placed, by his resignation, in an embarrassing situation. I felt confident that my endeavours, successful or not, to carry his instructions into effect would be favourably considered by him. To the indulgence of those who will probably form the new Government I have no claim. I should not have been selected by them to make known to Don Carlos the views of the English Government, and the manner in which I do so must be looked at by them with distrust. If I fail, as I probably shall, they will attribute my failure either to incapacity or to want of zeal.

This however is a selfish feeling, and one which I shall not allow to prevent my doing what I believe to be my duty.

The object of my mission is to put a stop to the effusion of blood, an object of which no

Government can do otherwise than approve. To delay the attainment of it might occasion the loss of many lives.

Moreover, acting as I am under instructions given by the Secretary of State for Foreign Affairs, I think that I am bound to proceed, unless I receive directions to the contrary from the same authority.

I have consequently determined to repair as soon as possible to the head-quarters of Don Carlos.

You will see by my despatch of this day's date that I have received a safe conduct from General Mina. I am in daily expectation of the return of the messenger to whom I entrusted the letters for the Count de Penne Villemur.

As soon as he arrives I shall set forth.

If you would take an opportunity of making known in the proper quarter my reason for coming to this resolution, I should be very much obliged to you. Pray accept my best thanks for the kind note which I received from you a few days ago, and believe me, &c,

ELIOT.

John Backhouse, Esq.,
  &c, &c, &c.

CONVENTION.

[TRANSLATION].

Stipulations proposed by Lord Eliot, H.B.M.'s Commissioner, and which will serve as a rule to the Commanders-in-chief of the belligerent armies in the Provinces of Guipuscoa, Alava and Biscay, and in the Kingdom of Navarre.

Article 1.

The Commanders-in-Chief of the two armies now engaged in hostilities in the Provinces of Guipuscoa, Alava and Biscay, and in the Kingdom of Navarre, agree to preserve the lives of all prisoners who may be made on one side or the other, and to exchange them as stipulated below.

Article 2.

The exchange of prisoners shall be periodical, twice or thrice in a month, or oftener if circumstances should require or allow it.

Article 3.

The aforesaid exchange shall be in exact proportion to the number of prisoners which each party shall present, and the number remaining over and above shall be retained by the party in whose power they are until another opportunity of effecting an exchange shall occur.

Article 4.

The exchange shall be made according to the rank.

Article 5.

If after effecting an exchange, one of the belligerents should require a point where he may be able to guard the prisoners who may not have been exchanged, it is agreed that, for their security and good treatment, they shall remain with, and be guarded by, the party in whose power they are, at one or more towns to be respected by the opposite party; the latter not being allowed to enter such towns, or in any manner to carry on hostilities against them whilst the prisoners remain in them: it being well understood, that in the towns where prisoners are kept, the manufacture of arms, ammunition, or military stores, shall not be permitted, and that such towns shall be selected beforehand by the agreement of both parties.

Article 6.

During the present contest, no person, whoever he may be, civil or military, shall be deprived of life on account of his political opinions, without having been previously tried and condemned in conformity with the Laws, Decrees, and Ordinances in form in Spain. This is only to be understood in reference to those who are not in reality Prisoners of War; for as regards them, the stipulations contained in the preceding Articles shall be binding.

Article 7.

Both the belligerent parties shall religiously respect, and leave in full liberty, the sick and wounded who may be found in hospitals, barracks, towns, farm-houses, or any other place; the sick having been previously recognized as such by the medical officers.

Article 8.

Should the war extend to other Provinces of the Monarchy, the present Convention shall be binding in them, provided that the armies, which, by the vicissitudes of war, carry on hostilities in them, be the same which are now engaged in hostilities in the three Basque Provinces and in the Kingdom of Navarre.

Article 9.

This Convention shall be strictly observed by the Commanders-in-Chief, on both sides, who may succeed to the command.

Head-quarters of Asarta.
April 26, 1835.
(Signed)

Thomas Zumalacarregui.

Eliot.

Head-Quarters of Logrono.
April 27, 1835.
(Signed)

Geronimo Valdés.

Eliot.

In the presence of J. Gurwood, Lieut.-Colonel in the service of H. B. M.

DIARY OF COLONEL GURWOOD.

(No. I.)

Diary of the Mission of Lord Eliot to Spain, with Notes.

1835

28th March.—Left London for Dover.

29th March.—To Boulogne, and en route to Paris.

30th March.—Arrived at Paris at 1 p.m., and dined with Lord Cowley.

31st March.—Dined with Lord Cowley, and proceeded to the South at 9.30 p.m.

4th April.—Arrived at Bayonne at 3 p.m.

5th April.—Dined with M. de Prat, the Spanish Consul, having waited upon all the authorities, military and civil, during the day. General Harispe not in Bayonne, but at his seat at Lucane, near St. Jean Pied de port.

6th April.—Visited the position of General Sir R. Hill at Mougerre, Ville-Franche, and crossed the Nive at the bac de Bellegarde by Chateau de Marac home.

7th April.—To Biaritz.

8th April.—To St. Etienne, Burial Ground of the Coldstream Guards, and to Boucaut.

9th April.—To Vieux Mougerre by the Adour, returned by Byng's Hill, dined with M. Paultier, the Sous Prefet.

10th April.—To Heramitz, Ustaritz, stopped by the Douaniers and Police, for not having passports with us—Basque church—General Harispe arrived —Serenade before his house.

11th April.—Arcangues, Jackass-hole, Garat's House, &c.

12th April.—Camp retranche.

13th April.—(Ministry out by newspapers)—By the banks of the Nive.

14th April.—Spanish officers from Oraa's Corps—At 10.30 p.m. received the required permission from Don Carlos to proceed to his head-quarters.

15th April.—Visited the Arsenal, new hospital, &c.—Foundations on 2 ½ metres of sand, which is encaisse by walls; sand wetted—Vauban's Magazine sunk bodily 4 feet—Wet sand of more than 2 ½ metres makes a foundation as solid as rock.

16th April.—At 3.30 p.m. to St. Jean de Luz; arrived at 6 p.m.—Reported to officer in command —Inroads of the sea—Socoa.

17th April.—At 6 a.m. to Behobie—At 8 a.m. proceeded from the bridge, escorted by the troops of the Queen of Spain, to Irun; received by the Governor, and proceeded with an escort of the regiment of S. Fernando to Oyarzun, short of which received by General Jauregui (El Pastor), and proceeded with him and his troops, posted en echelon on the road to Hernani; dined with him at 1 o'clock, and afterwards went on to Tolosa—Jauregui in the carriage with Lt.-Colonel Gurwood, and Lord Eliot in the cabriolet with his Staff-officer, Don Ignacio Empana; arrived at Tolosa at 4 p.m.— Ayuntamiento waited on Lord Eliot; reported that Don Carlos was at Onate, and Zumalacarregui at Cegama, with the whole of the Carlist forces. The force of Jauregui, independent of garrisons, consisted of four battalions, S. Fernando, Cacadores, Africa, and a battalion of Chapel Goristes, or Peseteros, so called for receiving one peseta per diem. Plenty of provisions, but the troops entirely confined to the towns, as Carlist bands are feared in the country between them. Both civil and military authorities complained of the outrages and cruelties of the Carlists. The Carlists and Christinos appear to understand each other's military merits. The Christinos garrison and defend, and the Carlists, not having guns, refrain from attacking towns defensible with musketry; this would be different with the contending armies of other countries. The battalions, seen to-day, carried only a havresac and appeared to be without necessaries—Jauregui, an excellent fellow, appeared straightforward, and much liked by the inhabitants.

18th April.—At 6 a.m. Jauregui (lodged in the post-house with us) paid us a visit—Proceeded with an escort on the road to Lecumberri: at about a mile from the town, the escort became alarmed at the report of 'Facciosos' being in the wood on the hill above the road, and retired upon us; we left them in this state, and proceeded to Assiba, where information was given us that the Junta of Navarre was at Lecumberri, waiting to receive us—At Lecumberri met Colonel Serradilla, whom Don Carlos had appointed to accompany us to his head-quarters—We dined with the Junta—Afterwards proceeded by the "Dos Hermanas" and Irurzun to meet the Colonel and the Junta at Echarri-Aranaz, to which they proceeded across the mountains—Passed the "Dos Hermanas"—The scenery from Tolosa to Irurzun fine and bold, mountains with snow, &c.— On arrival at Irurzun, garrisoned by the Queen's troops, saw Lieut. Turner, R.A., Aide-de-Camp to Lieut.-Colonel Wylde; he accompanied us to Echarren, where we found Lieut.-Colonel Wylde at the quarters of General Gourrea, whose troops appeared dirty and badly equipped. We were challenged very ridiculously at the outpost, not more than fifty yards from the village, in broad daylight. Gourrea appeared very ill. Proceeded by the Baranca, between two ranges of mountains, to Echarri-Aranaz, where we found Colonel Serradilla and the three members of the Junta of Navarre. Lieut.-Colonel Wylde accompanied us. We were lodged for the night in the Duke of Wellington's old quarters. Colonel Serradilla went off to Don Carlos. The village of Echarri-Aranaz bore the marks of the late siege: fortified houses, &c, all destroyed and desolate—The garrison of the place had been taken prisoners by Zumalacarregui, who went thence to Pampeluna, under escort; which escort, under some presence, just or unjust, were thrown into prison by Mina.

19th April.—7 a.m. Proceeded to the Venta of Alsasua; arrived there at 8. Two battalions of Carlists, one of Castile, and one of Navarre. Don Juan O'Donnel, and General Ituralde, second in command to Zumalacarregui. Dined, and at 12 proceeded through the country, in which Quesada had been defeated in April, 1834, by Zumalacarregui; thence to a pass and down a mountain to a valley in which Cegama is situated, there dined again, as Don Carlos had sent word that he would arrive at Segura to receive us. General Erro escorted us to Segura with about 20 lancers; great cries of "Viva Carlos V." among the peasantry. Arrived at Segura at 6. Don Carlos— Shortly afterwards saw two fine battalions, one of Alava, the other of Guipuscoa, apparently in good order; met Carvajal. Waited upon M. Cruz Mayor, Don Carlos's minister, at Don Carlos's headquarters. M. Cruz Mayor afterwards waited upon Lord Eliot, and sent an order that Lieut.-

Colonel Wylde, who remained at Alsasua, would be received by Don Carlos.

20th April.—Saw the two battalions march to mass. Don Carlos at mass at the church. At halfpast 11 Lord Eliot had his audience of Don Carlos, and gave him a precis of his instructions, which he had previously drawn up. Don Carlos received Lieut.-Colonel Gurwood afterwards, and expressed much gratitude for Lieut.-Colonel, Gurwood's attentions to his family "mi difunta mujer," and to his subjects at Portsmouth. M. Cruz Mayor conveyed to us the desire of Don Carlos to receive us at dinner; but that as Valdés' column had moved that morning from Salvatierra, probably towards Pampeluna, the "cuartel real" (Royal quarters) would probably have to move at a moment's notice; and he trusted that a more convenient day would occur to receive us. All the etiquette of a Court preserved at our reception. Sandals or alpargatas worn, instead of shoes, by the Carlists; saw an issue of shirts—On the heights in the evening, heard firing in the direction of VillaFranca—Lieut.-Colonel Wylde arrived from Eulate, to which place General Ituralde had conducted him, and where he saw Zumalacarregui, with his forces.

21st April.—Drew up the project of convention, for the exchange of prisoners, from the Duke of Wellington's instructions, and read it over to Cruz Mayor—Invited by Don Carlos to dinner—After dinner, conference with Cruz Mayor upon the convention: several alterations suggested by him and adopted; and several declined as inadmissible and contrary to the instructions. Don Carlos stated that if he could procure 50,000 stand of arms, in a fortnight he should have as many soldiers on the march to Madrid; but that France and England prevented this assistance; but still his means increased with his advantages; and as the Queen's Government had spent all the loan by anticipation, he did not doubt, unless they should be able to raise a fresh one, of eventual success, provided there were no armed intervention.

22nd April.—Conference with M. Cruz Mayor, and the general terms of the Convention approved of. Reports of fighting in the Amescoas; dined with General Erro and the officers of the staff. After dinner saw four battalions of Alava and Guipuscoa march past Don Carlos, when on parade, reported to me as 3000 men, this I doubted, and counted them as they marched past 2000. Mr. Turner, at my request, also counted them, and made the same number; they were very soldierlike, and apparently very enthusiastic. Firing said to be still continuing in the Amescoas.

23rd April.—Reports of the fighting of the two preceding days in the Amescoas, but no particulars communicated. Conference with Cruz Mayor, and the stipulations definitively settled, and approved of by Don Carlos, for Zumalacarregui's signature. At half-past two returned by another road to Alsasua. No particulars of the affairs in the Amescoas known, further than that Zumalacarregui had ordered 26 prisoners to be shot near Estella. The corrected copies of the Convention were to be sent to us afterwards, to the Venta of Alsasua. The three members of the Junta of Navarre, and Colonel Serradilla, came with us from Segura to Alsasua.

24th April.—Received at 10 a.m. the corrected Convention, from Cruz Mayor, and immediately proceeded by Olazagutia, and the "puerto," across the Sierra de Andia, to the "puerto" of Eulate, through a forest of beech. Table land of the Sierra of Andia, the scene of the actions of the 21st and 22nd. Descended the "puerto" into the vale of the Amescoas, to the village of Eulate, in the bottom of it. (Aranarache and Contraste up the valley)— Heard at Eulate that Zumalacarregui had left at 9 in the morning for Asarta. Lieut-Colonel Wylde and Mr. Turner for Estella—Valdés' Head-Quarters. We, accompanied by the Junta and Colonel Serradilla, proceeded by a very steep ridge of mountains, covered with Roble (oak), the guide taking us by the short cut, the best road being that from Aranarache—Arrived after much fatigue at the 'puerto' above Marque, the Carlist hospital station for the 'puerto,' saw Zuñiga and Santa Cruz. Passed through a forest of Encina (evergreen oak), and over the river Ega by a bridge,—the bridge at Arquijas being broken—Passed through Acedo, and arrived at 7 p.m. at Asarta—Received by Zumalacarregui at the door of his quarter—After a short time, left

Lord Eliot in an inner room with Zumalacarregui and Carlos O'Donnel. Colonel Serradilla having mentioned that 10 Christino prisoners, who had been brought in, had been ordered to be shot at day-light the following morning—Colonel Serradilla thought their lives might be spared at our intercession—I went into the inner room and mentioned the circumstances to Lord Eliot, who was explaining the terms of the Convention to Zumalacarregui and Carlos O'Donnel. Lord Eliot immediately requested Zumalacarregui to oblige him by sparing the lives of the prisoners—Saw Lord Eliot about a minute afterwards, who told me that Zumalacarregui had not hesitated an instant in granting his request, and had actually ordered that the prisoners might be acquainted with the change in their fate. They desired to be admitted to thank Lord Eliot, and Zumalacarregui sent them word that they should do so in the morning, before the troops: but they; having requested that they might do so directly, to which Zumalacarregui acceded, were brought up, nine in number. The serjeant threw himself on his knees, the others about doing the same, when Zumalacarregui told him to get up and thank Lord Eliot for having spared their lives. They then expressed their gratitude to Lord Eliot. It would be impossible to describe this scene, which, as a fiction on the stage, would very meagrely represent the reality. Zumalacarregui then said that he regretted Lord Eliot had not arrived the day before, as he would have spared the lives of the twenty-six shot at Barandeas. Hearing that Zumalacarregui had no spy-glass, and wishing to manifest our sense of his act of clemency, I requested Lord Eliot to allow me to give mine to Zumalacarregui, for whom I had first designed it, if I found anything to like in him. On the road, however, I had changed my mind, and intended giving it to Serradilla, whose kind attention to us called for some acknowledgment; but after this scene, Lord Eliot and myself thought I had better adhere to my first intention which I had just resumed. On presenting it to Zumalacarregui, before his officers, I stated that having heard he had no glass, I begged to offer him an excellent one, which perhaps might have additional value in his eyes, from having been used by the Duke of Wellington at the battle of Toulouse, and that its value would be still more enhanced by its being a memorial of his late act of clemency towards the unfortunate prisoners. He thanked me very much for it, and assured Lord Eliot and myself that he should appreciate it on both accounts; but he desired to declare to us that it was not his nature, and that he had no wish to put prisoners to death, but as the only mode of retaliation for the atrocities committed by Rodil and Mina, and other Generals of the Queen's Army, on the relations and friends of those who had espoused the cause of Don Carlos and joined his army.

Heard the details of the actions of the 21st and 22nd, and, making allowances for Spanish exaggerations, the following appeared to be the story.

It appeared that Valdés with thirty-one battalions, quitted Salvatierra on the 20th, and arrived at Contrasta, in the beginning of the valley of the Amescoas, for the purpose of attacking Zumalacarregui, who was with his forces at Eulate, but on arrival at Aranarache, the head of Valdés' column, instead of attacking Zumalacarregui, went up the Sierra de Andin, by the "puerto," either from design, or that they wanted courage to attack Zumalacarregui, posted at Eulate, in the valley, with 11 battalions. When the greater part of Valdés' column had got on the table land of the Sierra, by the "puerto" of Aranarache, Zumalacarregui attacked the rear of it, with three battalions, so as to harass the march. This had the intended effect, and the column of Valdés passed a cold night on the Sierra, whilst Zumalacarregui, with his troops, remained under cover in the villages below. The day following, Zumalacarregui attacked the flanks and rear of the column, with another battalion, in addition to the three, still keeping seven battalions in reserve. From the difficulties of the road towards Estella, particularly near Abarzuza, these attacks threw the column into confusion, which during the night, with forty or fifty partidas keeping up a continued fire, increased to a degree, that it was not till three in the morning following that Valdés' column arrived in Estella, where no provisions could be obtained, and the famished and tired troops were irregularly put up by thirty, forty, and fifty in different houses, where the owners were obliged to feed them. About 2000 under Colonel Vigo remained in a village until morning, when a force, collected by order of Valdés, under Cordova, proceeded there to bring them into Estella, which was done. It appeared that Colonel Vigo, by Cordova's account, had acted rightly in keeping his brigade in the village, as in attempting to enter Estella that night, he would only have added to the confusion. The column was obliged to march out the following day from Estella, towards the Ribera, to obtain provisions, as the magazines of Estella barely sufficed for the subsistence of the garrison and hospital. The reported loss in wounded appeared to have been about 300, the worst cases being left in Estella, the rest being carried with the column on mules, asses, etc., pressed into Estella—The killed, prisoners shot (twenty-six), and the wounded of Valdés' column, after two days severe fighting, and two battalions of Zumalacarregui, carrying all before them by the bayonet, could not be correctly ascertained, but on enquiry the number could not much have exceeded 400—But the state of demoralisation shown by the unwillingness of the Queen's troops to fight, as afterwards corroborated by Valdés and Cordova at Logrono, their plunder of Valdés' baggage and the epaulettes of their own officers in the dark, will tell a worse tale than a large list of killed and wounded. The chief loss, on the part of Zumalacarregui's troops, was in the battalion of Guias—his crack corps. One of Zumalacarregui's battalions, for a moment, got into confusion, which he put right by placing himself on foot with them, and by directing a diversion by another battalion. At supper, Zumalacarregui sat between Lord Eliot and Lieut.-Colonel Gurwood. Carlos O'Donnel, and Ituralde were present.

25th of April.—Conference between Lord Eliot and Zumalacarregui—Convention signed by Zumalacarregui—Mr. Heningsen, a fine handsome gentlemanly young Englishman, accomplished and speaking several languages, not nineteen years old, had been a volunteer and distinguished himself at Aranaz, for he had been made cornet of cavalry, and the cross of S. Fernando given him.—At ten, after chocolate, proceeded with Zumalacarregui, Ituralde, Carlos O'Donnel and all the staff to Mendaza, the corps of Guias drawn up in review—I rode with Mr. Heningsen, and learned much from him— Zumalacarregui has a general knowledge of the country and peasantry; but Ituralde a very minute and correct one—Everything depending on Zumalacarregui, who is both loved and respected by the whole army; violent occasionally in his language, but has a knowledge of character of the persons with whom he is so—The position from Mendaza to the hermitage, between Nazar and Asarta, covering Arquijas, very strong.

Entered a rich valley, La Berueza, covered in front by a ridge of hills from Monjardin towards Penacerrada. This ridge, on the top of which is the Convent of San Gregorio, is between La Sorlada and Los Arcos—Passed Piedramiliera and dined at Villa Mayor, thence proceeded to the Convent of Yrache—nuns—chocolate and dulces—Ituralde went forward to Estella, when the garrison soon took alarm and fired—Took leave of Zumalacarregui, Serradilla and the other officers, and requested Mr. Heningsen to write to Lord Cowley the details of events. The cries of "Viva Carlos V." everywhere, women dancing, and great enthusiasm on seeing Zumalacarregui—On arrival at Estella, great screeching of "Viva la Paz! Vivan los Embajadores! Viva Dios!!"—Sentry at the bridge, in the middle of the town, challenging and charging with his bayonet—Saw the Commandant, 2nd regiment (Queen's), six companies—the garrison, remainder at Viana—the other two battalions at Burgos—Fortified Caserne, gates, houses and places fortified—Ayuntamiento Hospital—Guard of Honour and band of music before our quarter—Franciscan friar—Entrance of Valdés on the 22nd, described as being in great confusion, and left for provisions on the following day in the Ribera—Great mystery or ignorance as to where Valdés was to be found— Illuminations in honour of Lord Eliot—Caution in conversation, police very strict, and no one permitted to walk the streets after dark—Streets although illuminated, quite empty; greater part of the young inhabitants in Zumalacarregui's army, said to be 800.

26th April.—The Commandant and Ayuntamiento at 8 a.m., with a guide and a merchant who came from God knows where; proceeded by the convent of Yrache to Los Arcos at 12—Fortified post, destroyed by Zumalacarregui. Great screeching of "Viva Carlos V! Vivan los Embajadores! Viva Carlos V! Muera la puta!" Dined at a person's house, who requested our influence with Valdés, to obtain the release of Don Zephirino Ores, and the Ama of Don Juan, the Chaplain with Don Carlos, he is in prison at Viana—By Sancol and Torres to Viana—Challenged by Sentry at the entrance of Viana—Lieut.-Colonel Wylde introduced us to Valdés and Espartero, the division marching out to parade, fine looking troops. Proceeded to Logrono, accompanied by an Aide-de-camp and the Commandant of Viana—Waited on General Cordova, and went with him to see his division on parade; saw the second Light Infantry, the battalion that shot Canterac at Madrid, fine looking troops— Cordova told me of the demoralized state of the army, complained of Valdés, his incapacity, and even of his personal conduct in the Amescoas, no arrangements about provisions, and great consequent disorganisation. From the long conversation with Cordova, it certainly proved very little in favour of Valdés, when reasoning on his departure from Salvatierra on the 20th;

and if the operations of the last week, from the relative stations of the respective armies, are to be a sample of what Valdés and his army are to accomplish, the result cannot be doubtful—The troops, however, whom I saw, showed no symptoms of insubordination, and one would suppose, had they been well commanded, would have made a more respectable debut—It was the opinion of Cordova and several of his officers, that nothing but the armed intervention of the allies could save the country from destruction—Cordova lamented this necessity, and told me that in the event of intervention he should resign; but he could no longer conceal from himself the absolute necessity of it—Cordova is evidently intriguing to save his easily earned reputation—He told me that he should go to Vitoria, and thence to Madrid—I was much surprised at all his disclosures; but his frankness does not prove his honesty: he may be in the pay of the French Government—On giving him my' opinion of the little I had seen and heard of Zumalacarregui he appeared surprised, and more determined in his decision of quitting the army—On returning to our quarter, I found Valdés and Basseria with Lord Eliot—Cordova read over the Convention, signed by Zumalacarregui on the 25th, and made several objections—The details canvassed article by article—the principle, however, acknowledged, and on remarking that Zumalacarregui would not desire better than that Valdés should withhold his signature to it, the copies were taken by

Valdés, for the purpose of signing, but at the same time, for pointing out the alterations he would wish to have made.

Cordova's division ordered to march in the direction of Haro and Vitoria.

27th April.—Cordova's division marched to Haro and on to Vitoria—Waited upon Valdés and canvassed the objections made by Cordova to the Convention—Lieut.-Colonel Wylde was with me—Explained the wish of Lord Eliot that Valdés should sign the Convention and write a memorandum upon each article which might admit of a doubtful construction, but warned them from making futile objections to words, which did not involve the principle; as any difficulty of the kind, manifested by them, would be turned by Zumalacarregui to his advantage, and to the prejudice of the Queen and her government in the eyes of Europe—Some warm expressions passed between Cordova and myself, as I found we were making no progress—In the course of the day the amended sketch was produced, of which I made two copies—Lord Eliot requested I would take them to Zumalacarregui for his signature, as the amendments he had thought proper to suggest in the original, signed on the 25th, which did not weaken the principle—Dined with Valdés at Espartero's—Valdés signed the original, as well as the amended copies of the Convention or Agreement—Cordova at dinner—In the amendments proposed, Cordova seemed to be the ostensible negotiator—Valdés said very little, Espartero less.

Tertulia in the evening—Valdés very civil and kind—I saw clearly that we had the power of dictating any terms consistent with the principle; but the suggestions made were certainly amendments, which rendered the Convention more clear, and satisfactory to the mediator, Lord Eliot.

28 April.—At 7 a.m. to Asarta over the mountains and snow; difficulty in preserving the track—Luckily, found Zumalacarregui—Going to dinner, previous to his marching away; his troops already on the move—Gave him the amended Convention and read over to him the original, already signed by him, and pointing out the alterations suggested—He said "No quiero hacer la guerra con palabras," (to quarrel about words), and as I see no alteration in the principle, already approved by Don Carlos, I shall sign it, which he did directly—I then pointed out that difficulties would occur in the details, and said that Lord Eliot had requested General Valdés to allow an officer of his (Zumalacarregui's) army to come to any given point to arrange them; for which purpose Valdés had given me a passport and I asked him to fill in the name. To this Zumalacarregui immediately replied, "Certainly," and going into the outer room, called upon Don Joaquin Montenegro to get ready to accompany me to Viana, or Logrono, or any other place I should point out; giving him a letter of

introduction to Valdés, and his instructions as to the places proposed in Article 5—At half-past 3 took leave of Zumalacarregui and proceeded with Montenegro to Logrono, by Ubago, Armananzas, etc., and arrived at 9; the weather had cleared up—I introduced Montenegro to Lord Eliot, and afterwards took him to Valdés, who received him with civility and kindness: Montenegro is an artillery officer (Mariscal de Campo) and had quitted Madrid only four months before to join Don Carlos. Valdés and the other officers consequently showed much good taste in their reception of Montenegro; a quarter assigned to him, and General Espartero gave him supper with me—Tertulia: conversation with La Vinda Coca, from whom I learned much of the state of parties in Spain. Twenty-two years ago I was lodged in her house; her husband is Governor of Logrono.

29th April.—Grand breakfast with Valdés, Espartero, Montenegro, Lieut.-Colonel Wylde, etc.: These breakfasts and dinners, with visits of ceremony and politeness, consume all that time which might be available for other purposes—Gave a list of prisoners to Valdés, who promised to release those named in it, now confined in Viana and Pampeluna, as also the escort who took the prisoners taken at Echarri-Aranaz, whom Zumalacarregui had released after the capture of that place—Valdés, with Montenegro, proceeded to Viana—I did not tell Valdés that Zumalacarregui was on the march.

30th April.—Finnessy, the messenger, dispatched at 5 a.m. for London vid Vitoria—Espartero left for Vitoria, to assume the command of the division of Cordova, gone to Madrid—Valdés, very civil, invited us to breakfast with him at Viana, on our way to Pampeluna; but on arrival at Viana at 10, found that he and his column had marched at daylight, in consequence of Zumalacarregui's previous movement—Overtook the column at Mendavia and breakfasted with Valdés; afterwards accompanied the column, 6000 infantry and four mountain guns, commanded by General Aldama, to Sesma—On arrival there took leave of Valdés, and went on to Lerin—Met General Lopes, who commands the cavalry—View from Lerin—Quartered in the same house with Lopes; joined him and his officers after tea; much exaggeration; most of them for intervention; of course, being cavalry of the guard, they preferred Madrid. San Miguel, the head of the staff of Valdés' army, and many others, decidedly against any armed French intervention. The mother of the Alcalde, in whose house we were lodged, quite a fiend respecting the Carlists, who, she hoped, would all be put to death, and their property destroyed.

1st May.—Saw Valdés' column marching on Lerin, crossing from Sesma—Lopes' Cavalry and two battalions of Infantry, one of Soria, the battalion of prisoners, turned out to be ready to march on arrival of Valdés—Six squadrons Carbineers, Lancers, and Cacadores of the

Guard, well mounted and equipped; two short six-pounders and howitzers—Valdés, San Miguel, etc., arrived. At seven a cold rain began to fall; went on to Larraga, where we left Colonel Wylde, and proceeded by Mendigoria to Puente de la Reyna—Rain incessant—Challenged at the gate—Soaked to the skin—Garrison consisted only of 36 Urbanos, in addition to convalescents of the line, the rest of the inhabitants had taken arms with Zumalacarregui—Said to be more than 600—Casa fuerte, in which the Urbanos and the known Christinos had slept during the last fourteen months.—Valdés arrived, civil messages from him. The infantry had stuck in the mud, lost their shoes, and arrived in a most pitiable state—We could not get on to Pampeluna—The Duke of Wellington's birthday—Stragglers arriving all night, three murdered by the inhabitants of Mendigoria.

2nd May.—Did not proceed to Pampeluna until 9 in the morning, in order that we might pass through the column, which marched at 6, to see the result of yesterday—Men in a sad state, wet clothes, and bad shoes, coughing, fever, etc.—Officers in the rear, with sticks, striking the men to make them keep up; the road excellent—Saw Valdés, who requested us to go on to Pampeluna, and sent an officer to Bendito, the acting Viceroy—Arrived at half-past twelve, and lodged in the Casa de Redin; found letters from Bayonne, and news of the formation of the new administration in England—Dined with Valdés; saw Sancho, Mina's favourite Staff Officer; much against intervention—At half-past six went to Mina at the Palace; received by him and Madame Mina—Mina evidently in bad health; his inactivity and the non-exercise of his military talents (if he ever had any more than those of a partisan), had done much injury to the Queen's cause during the last six months—His manner, an assumed mildness; but his conduct proved he was a wolf in sheep's clothing; against intervention, as are all his followers—Visited by Colonel St. Yon, the French Commissioner.

3rd May.—Visited Colonel St. Yon and the Portuguese attaché to the head-quarters—Visited the works and the Cathedral—Letter from Zumalacarregui, requesting intercession for a man and his wife confined in Pampeluna, whose son had joined his army and died—Dined with Valdés—Mendes Vigo arrived with the garrison of Irurzun, the siege of which had been raised—Valdés released the man and woman interceded for—Wrote to Zumalacarregui, and requested him to send us the dispatch, which Mina had forwarded to Lord Eliot (Lord Palmerston's), but which had been intercepted between Pampeluna and Puente de la Reyna, most likely by his people, and conveyed to him a message from Valdés to let fish pass, and he in return would allow wine to pass to his army. Took leave of Valdés, who in the transactions between us, appeared an honest man—I doubt his being a General. We had every reason to be satisfied with his attentions and kindness to us, as also the release of the persons confined; and had we received more empeños for the release of others, there is little doubt but that he would have acceded to our applications in their favour. Many still remained in prison in Pampeluna, who, of course, little knew how to call for the exercise of our influence over Valdés in this respect—Mina too unwell to receive us, took leave of Madame Mina— Lieut.-Colonel Wylde remarked the difference in the conduct of Valdés and Mina, and augured favourably as to his future position with Valdés. The garrison of Irurzun brought in to-day, having been besieged three days by Zumalacarregui; the Casa fuerte destroyed.

4th May.—At 7 a.m. by Villaba, Carlist post there (Sorauren Hill), Huarte, Zubiri—Taken before a Carlist post, in a gorge in the mountain; officer in command very civil; and proceeded with an escort, to prevent further detention, to Burguete, by Espinal: manufacture of powder— At Burguete, received by a Carlist battalion; the Colonel very civil and accompanied us to Roncesvalles, where we dined at 2—The Carlist forces here levy the duties on all merchandize from France—At 4, mounted the Puerto, by a short and easy ascent, and by Valcarlos (fine scenery) descended into France: four hours— Arrived at S. Jean Pied de port at 9; the officers at the French frontier being very civil—The Lieut.-Colonel of the 19th of the Line waited upon us on our arrival, with the excuses of Colonel Meslin, the officer in command, to whom we had announced our intended arrival from Roncesvalles.

5th May.—The Lieut.-Colonel waited upon us, and accompanied us to the Citadel, the Governor of which received us with much civility, but did not spare us a single bastion— Saw an extraordinary cavity in the vale below, where the extent of a circle, of about 80 or 100 yards diameter, had disappeared 30 feet deep to water, which was above 100 feet deep; a very extraordinary phenomenon—At 9.30 a.m., to Bayonne; arrived before 6, and waited on General Harispe, who was civil to us: he appeared, from late events and what I told him, not to be now very urgent as to French intervention, as he appeared to be before we had entered Spain—Very little of the actual state of affairs in Spain appeared to be known to him or any of the authorities; that would not be possible, so long as the only source of information, Colonel St. Yon, remains at Pampeluna, or at the head-quarters of the Commander-in Chief of the Queen's Army. He is not in a better position for obtaining information, respecting affairs in Spain, than Lieut.-Colonel Wylde—Saw Lagassiniere, Du Prat, M. and Mdme. Paultier (Sous Prefet), Mr. Harvey, etc.

6th May.—Saw the persons of the preceding day; Balasqeu, the mayor; and at half-past 4 went on to Orthes: arrived at n—I arranged with M. Paultier, the Sous Prefet, that my friend,

General Nunez Abreu, whom Don Carlos would not receive, nor permit to remain in, Spain, should obtain passports for wherever he might choose to go. I could not wait to see Abreu.

7th May.—At 6.30 a.m., to Pau—M. Leroy, the Prefet—Visited the chateau: balcony view of Jurangon, etc.—To Lestelle and Lourdes, Bagneres, &c.

8th May.—At 6 am., to Toulouse 5 p.m.— Mounted hacks and went over the position and field of battle—The redoubts all effaced; the Colomier still points out their several positions— Under the point of the great redoubt, above the village of Montblanc, where the Spanish columns failed, there is now a large establishment, the Ecole Veterinaire—Went to The Capitole— Bonaparte's bust replaced.

9th May.—At 6.15 to Montauban and Cahors; met Soult's son at dark—To Souillac at 1.15 a.m.; rough sheets and more dirt than in Spain as to every thing and place where cleanliness was required; eggs and oranges the only food free from it.

10th May.—At 6.30 a.m. to Brive, and Limoges at 9 p.m.

11th May.—At 7 a.m. to Chateauroux, and Vierzon at midnight.

12th May.—At 7 a.m. to Orléans and broke down, three-fourths of a poste from Etampes.

13th May.—At 7.30 a.m., carriage being repaired, on to Paris, and arrived at 12.30—Saw Lord Cowley, previous to his departure for London.

14th May.—In the evening waited upon Louis Philippe at the Tuileries, His Majesty having expressed a desire to see us: he first spoke separately to us, and M. de Broglie followed, asking many questions relative to the respective armies and the necessity of French intervention—When M. de Broglie left the chateau, the King conversed with us both together, for more than an hour; his object, he acknowledged, was to ascertain decidedly the necessity for an armed French intervention; whether it was desired, and what might chance to be the result of it—He stated that he, personally, was averse to an armed intervention, and that with that feeling only, had he been induced to become a party to the quadruple alliance, to avoid the necessity of an armed intervention, and that his ministers were of the same opinion. We stated, that without an armed intervention, there was not the most distant chance of a termination of the civil war; that several officers of the Queen's army, and all the authorities, who were committed to her cause, were for intervention of any kind, which might, by chance, turn the balance in favour of the Queen; but that there was also a very large number of officers of the Liberal party, as well as many other true Spaniards, as they call themselves, who deprecated all foreign intervention, as derogatory to the Spanish nation; and that the cause of the Queen, and that of the present order of things in Spain, was not worth support, if it could not stand without the aid of foreign armies—Louis Philippe then stated, that he was decidedly of that opinion, but from different motives; that the intervention must be for an indefinite period, if once it took place; and that he knew enough of the Spanish character to be satisfied that it could produce no ultimate good; that he could not spare the force which would be required, which, to be safe, must be very considerable; that the Chamber of Deputies would not vote the means to maintain it; and that whatever the intervention might cost would never be repaid by Spain; and that if called upon, by the present Government of Spain, for an army of intervention, which he was not bound by treaty to furnish, he should refuse it; and that he felt stronger in the propriety of his decision, from all that he had heard from us—Louis Philippe is quite right.

In concluding these remarks, it is a matter of personal gratification to make one, on the person under whom I was employed on this mission, and to state that the enduring patience, suavity of manner, clear perception, correct judgment, and many other rare qualities of straightforward diplomacy in Lord Eliot, offer every assurance that when a mission of greater importance shall be confided to his charge, he will not fail to employ his talents to the honour and advantage of the country.

LETTERS FROM COLONEL GURWOOD
TO LORD FITZROY SOMERSET.

Bayonne, 11th April, 1835.

MY DEAR LORD FITZROY,

We arrived here this day week, and are awaiting the answer to the communication made to Don Carlos, as also the "sauf conduit" of Mina, for which application was made by three different channels, the day after our arrival. We have been very fortunate in the weather, which has enabled us to visit the different parts of the positions of the army on the 13th, 14th, and 15th of December, 1813. We visited le petit Mouguerre, and the ridge of Ville Franque on the first day; Vieux Mouguerre and the banks of the Adour, on another, with the hill taken on the 15th, at the end of that day, by Sir John Byng's brigade. This gave Lord Eliot a clear view of the repulse of Soult's Army by Lord Hill's Corps. On another day we went to Biaritz, and from thence to Bidart, and the range of position towards Arcangues and Jackass Hole, which like Babylon, was only to be recognized by the painful recollection of where it once stood. On another day we visited Herauritz and Ustaritz, and were continuing our route to Cambo, when we were brought up by "les douaniers" and the police, and underwent interrogatories before Monsieur le Maire, who only spoke Basque—and on another day we visited Boucaut, and the ground of the sortie from the Citadel on the 14th of April, 1814, which it strikes me, must have been little creditable to those concerned in that affair. I had great pleasure in going over all these positions, the scenes of our former operations, inasmuch as I found all the impressions on.my memory completely verified: the only painful part was, that I found but very few alive, old enough to recollect the Campaign; and that I found some only, with the appearance of great age, who in the recollection of them, said "mais j'etais trop jeune alors pour m'en rappeler maintenant."

We are very well received here by the Authorities, and we pass our evenings with the Sous Prefet, whom I knew very well years ago at Paris; and through whom our sejour here has been rendered very comfortable. We expect to receive Don Carlos's answer to day, and if greater difficulties do not present themselves than we anticipate, we shall proceed to-morrow night on our journey to reach his head quarters. Lord Eliot, however, who combines great judgment with prudence, does not wish to pass the posts of the Queen's troops, on the frontier, by stealth, or in any manner inconsistent with his position, and has given notice of this intention to General Mina.

The different entrances from Irun to Zugarramurdi, are daily undergoing changes, as to the Carlists and Christinos who occupy the posts in them, and there is our difficulty. I have reason to believe that the Carlist predatory bands, on the frontier, would not offer much difficulty; but in the Queen's Army, there are bands under different leaders, who are but little under the control of Mina, and who act as light troops in the mountains, for the protection of the columns and convoys in the valleys of Bastan, Lanz, &c. Many of these are French, from the neighbourhood of St. Jean de Luz, and other parts of the French frontier, of the worst class of contrebandiers, and who rob, plunder, and murder all that come within their reach. These are called "Peseteros," from being paid one peseta per diem; and there are others called "Chappel Gorries," from their head dress being red caps. These are represented as being as bad. The last accounts of Don Carlos, were from Aranarrache, between Zuniga and Maestii, to which last place Zumalacarregui was laying siege: but to day it was said that he has quitted the Borunda, and that Zumalacarregui was at Lecumberri, near the pass of "Las Dos Hermanas," on the new high road between Tolosa and Pampeluna, which cuts into the road from Vitoria to Pampeluna at Irurzun. This movement of Don Carlos's General may have two objects in view—to clear the Frontier of the Christino posts I have mentioned, or to interrupt the progress of a very large convoy, now waiting at Ainhoa, to be conducted from thence to Elisondo and Pampeluna; and for which purpose, it is said that Mina is preparing another expedition from Pampeluna for its protection. Large reinforcements are said to have arrived at Vitoria, but from Christino authority I hear, that the greater part of these expected reinforcements have deserted, before crossing the Ebro, and that not one tenth part of the original number have reached Vitoria. Cordova is at Vitoria, commanding the Province, and it is said that Valdés, the Minister of War, is also arrived there, and that he will supersede Mina as Viceroy of Navarre—that is if Mina will permit it. There are various accounts of the state of Mina's health—some, that he is excessively ill—when the next bring news of his having mounted his mule to proceed on some expedition; but since our arrival here, I believe he has not quitted Pampeluna, although if well enough, he must either come, or send, for the convoy at Ainhoa.

M. Balasque, the Mayor of Bayonne, is the friend and agent of Mina, and between the two, a charge of 25 per cent, is said to be deducted "pour les fournitures et vivres ;" this, however, is the affair of the Spanish Government. Before Mina's Vice Royalty, Balasque supplied Zumalacarregui with arms, horses, &c. and may still do so for aught we know. There is no doubt of the fact that Don Carlos receives the greatest part of his supplies in arms, money, horses, and equipments from this very place. The greatest Carlist agent, M. de la Gassiniere, tells me that the whole of the means are furnished from Spain; this appears extraordinary; but what is still more so, is the fact that my friend the Sous Prefet, during the two months that he has been here, has repeatedly written to the Minister of the Interior of the existence here of a Junta of Carlists, in this very hotel St. Etienne; of their daily and even hourly communications with the Junta of Navarre, at Ezcurra near Zubiete; and that assistance of every description for Don Carlos, is afforded by this Junta, and others well known to the authorities here; and that no notice has been hitherto taken of it.

The whole of the villages, between the Adour and the Frontier, are crowded with troops. The artillery and heavy equipment of the Corps d'Armee, commanded by our old friend Harispe, are stationed here, at St. Jean de Luz, and sur la Grande route; and General Jacobi told us last night, that in twenty-four hours after the arrival of an order by telegraph from Paris, an army of 25,000 men could be thrown across the Bidassoa, and 20,000 more the day following. From what I can learn, the entrance into Spain would not be a popular service with the officers; to the soldiers, who, like all other troops, like changes, it would be more agreeable; but if the civil war should nevertheless continue, Zumalacarregui might with his forces (more numerous than those of Mina in 1810, 1811 and 1812) very much harass a French army occupying the north of the Ebro; for I take it that the inhabitants as well as the French troops are but little changed in their habits and feelings. However, there is no doubt of the readiness of the French Government to act as circumstances or interest may require. I see little difference in the French army—the same looseness of movement, the same description of pot gutted officers who carry their bellies in their breeches, the same rips of cast horses for their artillery, and cats for their light cavalry—the equipments of all arms appear to be nearly the same as in former days. With regard to the relative strength of the present belligerents, the Carlists and the Christinos, I am unable to judge; but from hearsay I am inclined to believe that the Carlist forces are increasing in numbers, as well as in enthusiasm; and that the army of the Queen's Government are not animated by any patriotic feelings proportionate to the Royalist feelings of their opponents. I doubt, as you must well know, the possibility of giving an accurate opinion on these subjects, even were I an actual observer; for one must be continually led astray by their bullying, boasting, and lying. Do not tell Alava this, or he will never forgive me. But so far as I am able to form an opinion, nothing but a French armed intervention can put a stop to the present barbarous warfare between the two parties; whatever may be the consequences which might hereafter attach to the party so intervening, or the results as to the coalition of the present contending parties in the provinces, as well as in the capital of Spain. That, however, is not our affair—and even the best digested plan, when the passions of men, as well as their prejudices, are concerned, nine times out of ten, have a very different result from that which was intended. All this, recollect, is from Bayonne. I have no personal authority for what I have not witnessed; and you must receive this as mere preliminary gossip, for what I hope to follow up with ocular testimony. For this reason I write to you, that you may read such parts of my communications to the Duke of Wellington as you may think proper, as I have not His Grace's sanction to write directly to him in this general way. Lord Eliot is so good as to acquaint me with the correspondence between him and His Grace, which leaves me nothing to add, so far as regards the object of the mission, farther than to express my feelings of gratitude for his confidence and partiality in employing me so agreeably, and where even the difficulties will increase the interest, and, if possible, my humble exertions to merit his approbation. My next, I hope, will be from the head-quarters of Don Carlos. We go armed across the Frontier, to prevent any failure in our mission by the interruption of it by common robbers—but to a regular armed force of any party we shall surrender at discretion, rather than risk the consequences of resistance. The plot thickens, but I have no doubt, as far as pen and ink go, we shall succeed in the humane object of the mission.

The fortifications of this town are being pulled down to be rebuilt, in such parts as may require it, on a more regular and extended scale—La Musique du 48me played a serenade last night before the house of the Colonel, on the Place d'Armes, it being his fete—St. Fulbert! Detroyat, master of our hotel, and who has much to do with the Carlist Junta, says, that notwithstanding the Christinos being on the Frontier, last night fifty ballots of saltpetre were passed over and received by the Carlists in the rear. M. de la Gassiniere has just put into my hands the enclosed states of the Carlist forces . in the provinces and Navarre and in Cataluna, as also the strength of Mina's troops according to the last returns.

Sincerely yours,

(Signed) J. Gurwood.

We have just received Mina's passport dated the 9th, in a very civil letter.

(No. 2.)

Bayonne, 15th April, 1835.

My Dear Lord Fitzroy,

Our departure from hence has been delayed by the non-arrival of the answer to the communication made by Lord Eliot to Don Carlos. The movements of the Christinos and Carlists, on the Frontier, prevented the return of our emissary until the middle of last night. A Lieut.-Colonel, with four battalions of Carlists, is waiting in the mountains, at Gorzueta, as an escort to conduct us to Don Carlos's head-quarters. This Lord Eliot has declined, and we have given the Lieut.-Colonel a rendezvous at a Carlist post "Las Dos Hermanas," beyond Lecumberri, on the road from Tolosa to Pampeluna, and we start from hence to-morrow for our destination, which we shall know on our arrival at " Las Dos Hermanas," or at Lecumberri. The Carlist Junta here believe Don Carlos to be at Barindano north of Estella, not far from Zuniga. Half a dozen officers of the Corps of Oraa, posted at Urdax came in here yesterday and expressed their satisfaction at the reported object of the mission—that of an exchange of prisoners. In this, however, they cannot be so much interested as the Carlist officers, for Zumalacarregui has not, for some time, shot any of the officers whom he has lately taken in arms. It appears that the Queen's Army have undergone great privations and fatigues, and there have been desertions from it into France in consequence. Mina's ill health, and the consequent expectation of his death or resignation, have not tended to advance the cause of the Queen in the northern provinces; and we hear reports of disorganization, or rather the want of proper organization, which certainly do not hold out hopes of the Carlists being put down by the Queen's Army. On the contrary, judging from report alone, and making allowance for Spanish exaggeration, one would be inclined to think that, from the Emprunt being expended, or rather squandered, without any apparent advantage to the Queen's cause, and the rebellion against it having increased, with an unabating enthusiasm on the part of the Carlists, there is little prospect of the civil war ceasing. General Harispe is, of course, of opinion that an armed French intervention would have that effect. As I do not pretend to be a prophet, I shall not presume to hazard an opinion with respect to the result of such a measure. I wrote last night, as also this morning, to Lieut.-Colonel Wylde with Lord Eliot's proposition to him to be at "Las Dos Hermanas" on Saturday next the 18th, agreeably to General Mina's suggestion, contained in Lieut.-Colonel Wylde's letter, which I enclosed to you in my last. In the beginning of next week it is hoped that the business of the mission will be arranged at Don Carlos's headquarters, which, if at Barindano, not far from Zuniga, will allow me to proceed from thence to Pampeluna in one day. Valdés is said to be on the eve of quitting' Madrid. He is to pass in review the Corps de Reserve stationed at Burgos; but whether he is to supersede Mina in the command of the Queen's Army in the Northern provinces, is not yet stated, if so, I suppose he will become the contracting party on the side of the Queen, to whatever may be arranged by Lord Eliot,with Don Carlos or Zumalacarregui. This may afford me an opportunity of seeing the

Queen's Army, and I shall endeavor to give you a detail of everything I see, and forward it by, the first safe opportunity.

    Sincerely yours,

       J. Gurwood.

The news from Madrid this morning mention that Mina remains Viceroy of Navarre, having resigned the command in the field, which Valdés succeeds to, Rodil holding the portefeuille de la guerre ad interim.

(No. 3.)
    Segura, 20th April, 1835.

My Dear Lord Fitzroy,

Since my last letter to you, of the 15th, No. 2, we have quitted Bayonne, and by a very roundabout route came here last night, where Don Carlos arrived from Onate, about an hour afterwards. As I keep a memorandum of our proceedings, in the chance of your taking the trouble to read it, I send you a copy; although I fear you will be unable to form any accurate opinion of this state of civil war, which defies description; but, at all events, it will be as correct, with regard to facts, as any other; whenever I give an opinion, you will be the best judge of its justness. From the advantages derived by a regular government, with troops and money at command, the army of the Queen, one would think, ought to have put an end to this civil war; but as experience has proved the contrary, it is natural to guess at the apparent causes of the failure hitherto. These I must jumble together, and in doing so, must in some measure have recourse to the opinion of others, as well as reports which may be unjustly founded. I cannot discover, in the first place, that the mass of the Spanish nation has made any great strides since I was last in this country, in the knowledge of the advantages of constitutional government. In the second place, there is little confidence placed, by those few who do comprehend the advantages of a liberal government, in the ministers who have to carry it into effect. Thirdly, the Army, which has seldom been known to be in a good state of discipline, is, I should say, from what I have rapidly seen of two corps, Jauregui's and Gurrea's, worse than ever—badly composed and miserably equipped. The general officers commanding are, apparently, not much respected; and, from the want of all professional talent, are unlikely to work any change to the advantage of their reputation, or that of the troops under them.

These are my opinions as to the causes of the failure of the Government to put down the rebellion. The next things to consider are the causes of the support of the rebellion against the Government. To all who know Spain and the Spaniards, they will be apparent. There is a respect for the old, hitherto legitimate, authority of their Kings, among the mass of the nation, of which nine-tenths are under the influence of the priesthood. This influence has undergone little or no diminution among the lower class, who are the fighting part of the nation; it may have undergone a great change among the talking part of it, but not to the extent to cause the substitution of any other influence in place of it. Secondly, there is a national enmity in the Navarrese and Provincials to any Government that would interfere with their fueros or privileges, which the Government of the Cortes have manifested a desire to set aside, particularly when they know that there is not power sufficient to do so. Thirdly, there is an enthusiasm for Don Carlos, among all the inhabitants of the villages and open country, which the peasantry feel for their kings, and which is increased by what would probably have a contrary effect in other countries—his strict and constant attention to all his religious duties. Fourthly, there is very great enthusiasm among his battalions, and the officers are animated by great zeal and activity, and their Generals, particularly the General-in-Chief, men who have given proofs of their professional intelligence and talents. These I take to be the causes of the success of this rebellion in the Northern Provinces against the Queen's Government, and which, if not prevented from receiving aid from France and England, would very shortly destroy it; for if supplied with 20 or 30,000 stand of arms for the numerous volunteers now without them, no forces of the Queen's Government could prevent the Army of Zumalacarregui from marching direct to Madrid. It is quite extraordinary to see what has been done, and is still doing, in arming and equipping, notwithstanding every attempt to prevent supplies being furnished from France and England. The country, the seat of war, is all cultivated, and the crops growing as in time of profound peace; the flocks and cattle in the mountains very numerous, and if left to themselves, as far as one can judge from what has hitherto happened, the Civil War may last for years, as the Carlist forces can supply themselves with provisions from the valleys, in the different ranges of mountains, in which the Queen's Army fear to trust themselves. The war here is a repetition of that of Mina against the French from 1810 to 1813, with as little chance of any other result. The intervention of an armed French force might perhaps have a great influence, if the French Army paid for its supply; otherwise its success in interference, I think, would be very doubtful. The same spirit of enmity to Frenchmen exists among the lower orders, and the same excesses would be committed on them as are now committed by the Queen's Army towards the Carlists, when they fall into their hands. (12 o'clock.)—Lord Eliot has just had his formal audience of Don Carlos. I believe he will consent to agree to the principle of the Cartel, although I suspect there will be a difficulty in the details. Don Carlos would have asked us to dinner, but it was not then known whether he would not have been obliged to quit this at a moment's notice, as Valdés was last night at Alsasua, on the road to Pampeluna; and he might have turned towards this place. Zumalacarregui is in the Amescoas, on the south side of the route from Vitoria to Pampeluna. The defence of these countries by a small force, is by no means difficult, and the communications are seldom longer than eight hours at the extreme points. Their information is very rapidly communicated and never interrupted, whereas, not above one-half of the Christino correspondence reaches its destination. I should like to be on the high road, as something must occur shortly.

Sincerely yours,

(Signed) J. GURWOOD.

7 p.m.—Colonel Wylde, for whom Lord Eliot obtained a "sauf conduit" from Don Carlos, to come to pay his respects to him, has just arrived here. After we left him at Alsasua, yesterday, General Ituralde marched to the Amescoas, and Colonel Wylde went with him and saw Zumalacarregui at Eulate. I believe the whole Carlist force to be assembled there. On returning to Alsasua, to receive Lord Eliot's answer, he met, at Olazgatin, the advanced guard of Valdés, the officer commanding which, at the moment,

received an order to retire, as he intended to follow Zumalacarregui to Eulate, and attack him wherever he should find him. Should this be the case, and the Christinos act on the offensive, we may hear of a battle tomorrow, unless all ends as is usual in Spanish affairs. Colonel Wylde says, that Zumalacarregui desired him to inform Lord Eliot, that he should accede to the Cartel with great pleasure, and release prisoners, even on parole. This appears quite in accordance with the feeling here—therefore no difficulty will exist to the proposal here. I fear, from a proclamation of Valdés, that I have just seen, that it will not be in accordance with his views; it is dated Vitoria the 18th of April, and denounces the rebellion with vehemence—Lord Eliot will forward it. We shall perhaps hear to-morrow* the result of Valdés movement on Las Amescoas. Lord Eliot and myself, when on the height above this, an hour ago, heard in the direction of Villa Franca, a very heavy "tirateando," said to be of the partidos on the river beyond the Sierra. 8 p.m.—I have just come from El Palacio. News has been brought from Salvatierra, that Valdés and the whole of his force, 17 or 18 battalions, had returned to that place, and put up there. I suppose that the fight is postponed.

See Extract from Diary, page 75.

(No. 4.)
Segura, 22nd April, 1835.

My Dear Lord Fitzroy,

Lord Eliot has finished his affair here, and we leave this to-morrow for the head-quarters of Zumalacarregui for his signature to the Cartel, and from thence we shall go to that of Valdés. We do not know exactly where are the head-quarters of either, as they have been fighting, during the last two days, in the neighbourhood of Eulate, in the Amescoas, with what result we know not. Four battalions marched past Don Carlos this afternoon. It would be difficult to give a description of their military appearance, one of them has been formed only during the last month; but there is an air of enthusiasm about the whole, which Lieut.-Colonel Wylde says does not exist among the Christinos. This I can readily imagine, as the Christinos are said to desert wherever they can get away, whereas the Carlists only want arms to form battalions, there being about 8000 Navarrese anxiously waiting to enrol themselves. I believe we shall get to-morrow to Salvatierra, if Valdés should be there, but it will be much easier first to get to Zumalacarregui, if in the course of the ride to Alsasua, which is on the high road, we should discover where he is. We have, however, no difficulty in going from one post to another, and are respected by both parties. It is Lord Eliot's present intention to remain at Bayonne, after having effected the object of his mission, and sent off the result of it to the King's Ministers, there to await any further instructions that they may think necessary to send him. In the meantime, awaiting orders, we shall go to Vitoria, Pampeluna, Pau, &c.

Sincerely yours,
(Signed)   J. Gurwood.

(No. 5.)

Asarta, Head Quarters of Zumalacarregui,
April 25th, 1835.

My Dear Lord Fitzroy,

Since I last wrote to you, from Segura on the 22nd, we have been on the move. We slept that night at the Venta of Alsasua, and yesterday morning, having received the corrected copies of the Cartel, we started for Zumalacarregui's headquarters. We mounted the Sierra de Andia, by the puerto of Olazagutia, and crossed a table land to the puerto of Eulate—valley of the Amescoas, and the scene of the actions of the 20th, to the 22nd. Valdés, with thirty battalions, had entered the Amescoas, in three columns, by Contrasta, &c, but finding Zumalacarregui stationed, with eleven battalions, between Aranarrache and Eulate, and St. Martin, he went up the puertos to the table land of the Sierra Andia. In this operation Zumalacarregui attacked his rear and flank with four battalions, leaving the remainder of his forces in the valley as a reserve. The continuation of Valdés' march towards Estella being thus interrupted, for the sake of his rear-guard, he was obliged to bivouac that night on the table land; the day following, as far as I can make out, a similar attack was made by Zumalacarregui on their rear-guard— no prisoners were made, and there being much confusion among the young soldiers in Valdés' column, there was, according to reports, a great, though unequal slaughter—the Carlists in their attacks not having suffered much. The fact of Zumalacarregui having had only four of his battalions in action may account for this, and speaks largely for Zumalacarregui's prudence and generalship. A body of about 2000 of Valdés' column was cut off from Estella, near Artaza, but succour from Estella, on the 23rd, conveyed them in. As I before said no prisoners were made; about five-hundred stand of arms have been brought in, and the day before yesterday, fifty prisoners, found in the mountains, were shot. So much for the battles. On arrival yesterday at Eulate, we heard that Zumalacarregui had left it for Asarta, to be near his favorite position of Arquijas, and we proceeded across two ridges of mountains, one more steep than the other, and totally impracticable for any other troops but the Navarrese, of which this part of the Carlist army is composed. We arrived here at about seven last evening, having, on our way, passed the villages in which the hospitals and Carlist Depots are stationed. It would be quite impossible to describe the magnificent scenery of these mountains, accessible only by narrow paths and difficult passes. How Zumalacarregui manages to march eight and ten leagues a day, receiving communications from every part of his command throughout Navarre, I cannot comprehend. He has shown great talent, for he only fights when sure of advantage. There is also an enthusiasm among his troops, and particularly among his officers, which is quite incredible, when you know that certain death awaits not only them but their families, according to what has occurred. In the room in which I am now writing, there is one of the Junta of Navarre, whose whole family is in prison, one of them having been shot. But as I have neither time nor space for many details I should otherwise enter into, I must proceed with our reception at Asarta. Zumalacarregui received us at the door and shewed us up stairs. Here we were introduced in form by Zumalacarregui to the several officers of the staff collected—General Ituralde, O'Donnell, etc., whom we had seen on the 19th, at Alsasua. You may figure to yourself Zumalacarregui, as being in shape something like Colonel Barclay, of the 52nd, or rather stouter than Sir Colin Campbell. A very fine head, something resembling the heads of Christ, or the heads of Jupiter, excepting rather wider in the forehead, with large well-formed eyebrows, and large hazel eyes; his whiskers and moustachios joining—but the chin, and all on a level with his mouth, shaved quite clean; his forehead and nose quite Grecian and in a straight line; the whole forming a very fine head; there is no expression of ferocity, but of great penetration and intelligence; his uniform, like all the officers, being the Zamarra, or black sheepskin pelisse. Ten prisoners had just been brought in and directed to be shot. This operation usually takes place at daylight; therefore Lord Eliot thought it very opportune to request that their lives might be spared, using arguments as creditable to his judgment as to his proper feeling.

Zumalacarregui immediately accorded the request, and you may conceive the result to the poor wretches who, when they heard it, desired to present their homages to the Embajadór Ingles. The scene was not to be described. They were poor miserable Andalusians, who lost much in comparison with the Navarrese, who were the guard. Zumalacarregui did the whole thing in a very frank, honorable and manly manner; and only regretted that Lord Eliot had not arrived the night before, that he might have had the pleasure of sparing the lives of the other fifty, who had been shot by his order, which the conduct of the Queen's troops towards the inhabitants of the villages, occupied in the Amescoas by the Carlists, had demanded. His whole conduct was very conciliatory, and I thought it a good opportunity, with the consent of Lord Eliot, to present him with my glass, which I told him might not be unacceptable to him, from having been used by the Duke of Wellington at the battle of Toulouse, as well as a record of his clemency in acceding to Lord Eliot's request. The whole had a good effect, and if the mission has no other result, there is still the satisfaction of ten men's lives having been saved by Lord Eliot's interference. This was followed by supper, and we passed the night very gaily. I slept in a small room with two fellows whom I should not like to be my bosom companions. This morning at seven, Lord Eliot obtained the signature in duplicate of Zumalacarregui to the Cartel, and everything has gone on well. This morning I have met with a very gentlemanly young man, Mr. Heningsen, who is in the cavalry, and who by his gallantry has been made Alferez in the cavalry, with the first-class of S. Ferdinand. He is a very fine looking fellow, about nineteen— excellent manners and speaking French and Spanish very correctly. His manners would do credit to a cornet of the Life Guards, or the Blues. I never was so taken with any one. He tells me that every thing depends upon the General, and if any misfortune should deprive the army of him, the whole thing must go to ruin. In the action the other day, part of his troops got into confusion; he immediately, by bringing up another battalion, re-established order, and carried on his success—but none but himself could have done it. The force of Valdés was about 12,000—that of Zumalacarregui about 6000, of which not above 1500 were in action. The loss of Valdés is supposed to be about 700. Five hundred muskets have been brought in, picked up on the field—but more were on the ground, which they had no opportunity of carrying off. The action ceased only at the walls of Estella, from whence a fire prevented further pursuit. After the action the Carlists occupied fourteen villages, and Valdés the town of Estella, from which not a man dares move unless in large bodies; a small detachment would be directly cut off. At eleven o'clock Zumalacarregui accompanies us to Estella, and as Mr. Heningsen is allowed to accompany us, I have no doubt I shall hear more which may interest you.

Your's, &c.

(Signed)   J. Gurwood.

Villa Mayor, below Mont Jardin—2 p.m., 1 hour from Estella. Zumalacarregui has accompanied us as far as this, and he will only quit us within gun shot of Estella.

(No. 6.)

Logroño, Monday, April 27th, 1835.

My Dear Lord Fitzroy,

My last, of the 25th, No. 5, left us going into Estella. The greater part of the town is turned into a fortification, by means of gates, loopholes, &c. We were received by the inhabitants screeching "Viva la Paz" till our heads ached with their piercing screams.

Part of the 2nd regiment (Queen's) formed the garrison; the army, with General Valdés, had quitted it the day after their arrival, for Lerin, and the other towns in the Ribera, where they could obtain provisions, as the stores of Estella could afford none, without endangering its safety. The town, with the exception of the Ayuntamiento, was all Carlist. The Commandant of the garrison, as well as the Ayuntamiento, waited upon us, but could give us no account of General Valdés or the army. The severest police is enforced, and no one is permitted in the streets after dark; and although an illumination was ordered in honor of Lord Eliot's arrival, no one could remain in the streets to see it, and the honor smoked away in solitude. On the following morning, on proposing that we should proceed to Mina at Pampeluna, we were told that we might possibly find Valdés at Viana or Logrofio. At eight therefore we proceeded there, via Los Arcos; on arrival at which place, our ears underwent an incessant screeching of "Viva Carlos V.! Vivan los Embajadores Ingleses, Viva Carlos V.!" the women dancing and screaming the hour we remained there. On the road, we constantly saw mules, laden with bread and wine, coming in from the Ribera and going to the Carlist villages. At Sancol and Torres, the screams of Carlos V. were repeated; and at about four o'clock we arrived at Viana, where we found one division of Valdés' column, said to be 7000, and that general's head quarters. As His Excellency proposed going to Logrofio in an hour, we continued our route there. I saw the division marching out to parade, close to Viana, and, although not to be compared either to French or Portuguese, appeared to be well armed and equipped; the sac, not the mochilla, appeared almost empty of any necessaries, and therefore very light—they were equally dirty. On arrival at Logrono, I waited on General Cordova, and went on parade with him, to see his division, which he reported to be more than 7000. I guessed them at five, and believe I was above the mark. Cordova, whom I knew some years since in Paris, detailed to me the whole of the proceedings of the preceding week, from the time of leaving Vitoria and Salvatierra; and really, for the march of an army of a civilized country, the detail of it was very amusing to me. The object of Valdés, in quitting Vitoria, was to attack Zumalacarregui, and destroy the villages, in the valley of the Amescoas, where Zumalacarregui was posted.

On arriving, however, at Eulate, in the middle of the valley of the Amescoas, instead of attacking Zumalacarregui, he directed the head of his column up the puertos to the table land above: with what intention, Valdés alone knows; but in carrying this operation into effect, Zumalacarregui attacked his rear and flank with four battalions, keeping nine in the valley below, as a reserve in the villages, whilst Valdés' army were kept "al fresco" on the top of the mountain table land! The march of the column was continued the day following, and was again attacked by Zumalacarregui, in a strong pass, until the whole marched into Estella, in the greatest confusion, from seven in the evening until three in the morning, in total darkness, through a difficult, mountainous and woody country, without an atom to eat!! The troops lodged themselves by fifty or sixty in the different houses in Estella; the inhabitants of which had orders to feed them. Cordova corroborated to me the report I had heard at Estella, of the complete state of disorganization of Valdés' column; although he states their loss at 150 to 200 men only, after two days' hard fighting! both of which are compatible in a Spanish Army. Thus, it would appear, the first object of Valdés—the attacking Zumalacarregui—quite failed. I cannot discover what other object he could have had, for on his arrival at Estella, he proceeded to Lerin, and marched the day following to Viana and Logrono; and this day, one division marched from this to Haro; and, of course, that from Viana must follow the movement, as Zumalacarregui will fall upon them, if they attempt to move separately. On looking over the map, you will find it a very odd week's work; and if this promenade be a sample of what is afterwards to be done by Valdés, you may, I think very shortly, hear of the break up of the army, or his dismissal. Nothing but an entire failure can be the consequence. The troops, however, which I saw yesterday, from appearance and equipment, one would have thought, might have made a more respectable debut in the affair of the Amescoas, where the General had the choice of position and attack; and it will be very difficult to calculate upon any success against Zumalacarregui, in any position which he may take up for the defence of his valleys. The enthusiasm of the troops under Zumalacarregui is certainly great; and Valdez has evidently lost all hope of making any impression, even when he has the choice of position and attack. Zumalacarregui now has his battalions feeding in the villages, from the gates of Estella to Viana. His advanced position which he will occupy in the event of being attacked, in front of Arquijas, his left on Mendoza and right on Asarta, for the defence of which he has plenty of troops, and other positions of less extent, in his rear towards Arquijas, to fall back upon in case of not maintaining his first would appear to set Valdés at defiance; and the present reported inefficient and demoralized state of the Queen's troops, now withdrawn to a distance, adds much to the moral effect which the advantages, however insignificant they would be in other armies, obtained by Zumalacarregui in the late operations, has produced in the troops under his command. From this detail you will see that Valdés has completely failed, both as a soldier and as a commissary, and there is an evident feeling, and I think also a wish, on the part of the General Officers Commanding the Queen's Troops, that an armed intervention of the Allies is absolutely necessary; although their present numerical superiority and professed contempt of the enemy should have an opposite tendency.

10 p.m—We dined with Valdés to-day—there is a hitch in the Convention—only stupid Spanish technicalities—but Lord Eliot wishes not to urge Valdés, and I shall quit this at daylight to-morrow, with new papers for Zumalacarregui's signature at Asarta, to return here the day following and enable Lord Eliot to send off the messenger with the whole of the documents complete, by Vitoria,

to Bayonne. Lord Eliot and myself intend to go from hence to Pamplona, by the Ribera, and by Roncesvalles to France. The Government, into whatever hands it may have fallen, cannot find fault with the want of success of the mission, nor with any want of zeal, diligence, activity and perseverance, in those who have endeavoured to carry it into effect. To have to do with smoking Spaniards is always difficult, but to have to do with two sets of them who think of nothing but how to devise a difficulty is quite an abomination. Cordova is going off to Madrid; he will trip up Valdés' heels, and I foresee nothing but chaos. Valdés receives bad news, and demands from all quarters of assistance. I could write an hour more upon the lamentable consequences of last week, without saying more than is true, as to the apparent result. I go to Zumalacarregui with a good grace, as Valdés has released the escort from Echarri Aranaz, whom Mina put into prison at Pamplona, and two old women of Los Arcos, whom Lopez put into prison at Viana. I shall send this off to Lord Cowley as usual.

Sincerely, &c,

(Signed) J. Gurwood.

There are great illuminations and ringing of bells to-night, in honor of Lord Eliot.

Tuesday, 28th April, 2 p.m.

I have just arrived at Asarta. Zumalacarregui has signed the convention, as altered by Cordova and Valdés, without difficulty. I luckily came here in time before Zumalacarregui marched, which he does in an hour. I have had a terrible ride this morning; seven hours over mountains covered with snow, and snowing so much that I could hardly see my way. The weather is terrible, and roads dangerous; but I hope to get back to-night to Logrono, as Lord Eliot is anxious to send off the messenger with the Convention.

Excuse this, but I am chilled with the cold and tired. Zumalacarregui behaves like a king.

Sincerely yours,

(Signed) J. Gurwood.

P.S.—It snows in these mountains to a degree quite extraordinary. I have six hours daylight, and I have no doubt shall arrive safe at Logrono, in spite of weather and all the armed parties on the road. Zumalacarregui is in the highest spirits, and is about doing something, as all his troops are on the move.

J. G.

Logrono, April 30th, 1835.

My Dear Lord Fitzroy,

I sent you from Asarta, the day before yesterday, letter No. 5, to the postscript of which I have little to add. I remained three hours with Zumalacarregui who sent with me Don Joaquin Monte Negro to Logrono, to arrange the details of the Convention with Valdés, who received him very well on his arrival, and yesterday after breakfast they both proceeded to Viana. We remained until this morning to dispatch the messenger off to London, by Vitoria, Tolosa, &c, and shall proceed after breakfast, by Lerin, to Pamplona, where we intend to pass a day, and return to Bayonne by Roncesvalles. We hope to be in Paris by the 1oth of May; by way of change we take Pau, &c, on our return. Cordova left this for Vitoria, the day before yesterday, to join his division there. I am told that, as he intends going to Madrid, Espartero is to succeed him in his command. Aldama commands the other division stationed at Viana, to which place Valdés moved his head-quarters yesterday. The impotent campaign of this army, even judging from their own reports, speaks sufficiently to render any further attempts hopeless, although I heard last night, from an old friend here, very intimate with Valdés, that he intends to make another effort to burn the villages in the valleys of Zumalacarregui. Should he not succeed, he will then, much against his inclination, he says, do his utmost in recommending the armed intervention of the French, with the hope of saving the country from complete anarchy. I doubt whether this result can be averted. The Carlist party, except in Navarre and the discontented parts of some of the provinces, is notoriously weak, and he will find the same difficulty in subduing all those who have compromised themselves since the death of Ferdinand, as the Queen's Government has the exalted Royalists in Navarre. Should Don Carlos unfortunately succeed, the Civil War will be more severe than even at the present moment, and anarchy must in this case be the result. In fact, I see no daylight anywhere for this unfortunate country. The money spent during the last year, to put down this rebellion in the north, shows that the present Government cannot avert this alternative, and there is quite sufficient experience that the revolutionary and republican parties in any country afford no other. I heard last night that Zumalacarregui put the ten men he pardoned, at the request of Lord Eliot, to death, soon after we quitted him. This I cannot believe, for I think I should have heard of it the day before yesterday, and Montenegro, who is a Mariscal de Campo, would have scarcely trusted himself either here or at Viana, if such had been the case. But it is impossible, among all the swaggering and lying of both parties, to discover the truth. Lord Eliot has requested me to make out a resume of my observations, addressed to him, that he may transmit it to the Government. I shall do so if I can, but in reality, in this chaos of all that is .Spanish, it will be difficult to make any statement which would be satisfactory to myself, and I should doubt my opinions being acceptable when they would afford no hope. His own separate dispatch of yesterday's date is a very clear statement of affairs to which I, as a soldier, could add but little, and that little would be doubtful as an authority by which the opinions of those who know nothing of Spain and Spaniards are to be guided. All the sick and wounded capable of being moved are brought on here by the column from Estella. There is a good hospital establishment here and the country being open to the Rioja, favourable for supplies. I have just heard that we are to undergo another Spanish breakfast this morning at Viana, with Valdés, the one yesterday nearly killed me; it is literally dining at nine in the morning, which consumes two hours, and what with their breakfasts, dinners, and cigars, one really cannot get a moment for important occupation. Notwithstanding all this I shall have passed a very pleasant month with Lord Eliot, although in going to Zumalacarregui the day before yesterday, over the mountains, and from snow not being able to see twenty yards before me, among precipices, I more than once wished myself at home. On more than one occasion I became very religious, and let drop the reins on the beast's neck trusting to his instinct and Providence; the descent into the valley made me forget everything again, excepting the commission with which I was charged, and I returned to Lord

Eliot the same night at Logrono to his great surprise. The season here is without a parallel in the memory of the inhabitants, and, excepting in the valleys, the season is as backward as when we left England, now a month since. All the Spaniards here are sitting round the brasero folded in their cloaks.

Sincerely, &c,

(Signed) J. GURWOOD.

Puente de la Reyna, 1 May, 1835.

MY DEAR LORD FITZROY,

My last letter (7) from Logrono, by Fennessy, the messenger, left us the morning of our departure for Pamplona on the 28th. The column of Valdés had left Viana, and we overtook it at Mendavia, where we breakfasted with Valdés, and proceeded with him and his column as far as Sesma, where they halted for the night. We went on to Lerin, where we fell in with the cavalry under Lopez. The march from Mendavia to Sesma with the column of infantry, which was called 8000, was rather interesting. I should say, that 6000 was nearer the number. They marched with a large front of Companies, and kept well up—the baggage, &c, being on the reverse flank, marching right in front: there were four guns carried on mules. The men were all in great coats and well equipped, in comparison with the troops of Zumalacarregui, but very indifferently, in comparison with other armies that I have seen. Not a man was left behind on the march from Viana to Sesma: had such been the fate of any man, in all probability he would have been picked up by the Carlists' Partidas or Aduaneros, in less than an hour after the column had passed. The force under General Lopez at Lerin, which turned out this morning to precede Valdés' column to this place, consisted of two battalions of infantry, and six squadrons of Cavalry, the Lanzeros, Casadores y Carbineros of the Guard, each squadron about forty file, which might, with the eclaireurs, advanced guard, &c, be calculated together at 600 men at the outside. There were two short six-pounders, and two howitzers with this force, in all about 2000 men.

As Valdés' column arrived at Lerin, Lopez marched from it. This was about 7 this morning. It soon after began to rain—the road became a thick paste, through which we slipped as far as Larraga, where Valdés had ordered breakfast;

but as Lord Eliot and myself were wet through, we left word that we should proceed to Puente de la Reyna, and to Pamplona in the afternoon, if it should clear up. However, no such good fortune awaited us, and an incessant rain brought us up here as wet as fish. Valdés arrived about five, bringing in Lopez' column, and leaving his own at Larraga. This day's march can only be compared to that of Beresford's brigade, on the Ezla, in 1808— the road was one sheet of mud, the greater part of the men's shoes being left in it, and I question much their being able to get to Pamplona tomorrow. As the troops have no change of clothes of any kind, I have little doubt but the greater part of those, who are not animated by patriotism, will endeavor to get into the hospital at Pamplona. We were lodged last night at the same house at Lerin, with General Lopez—an active intelligent young man. We passed the evening with him and his officers—who, like the officers of cavalry in other services, spoke much, but to little purpose, on the campaign. I was rather surprised to hear several of them despairing of doing anything, and confessing that without foreign intervention they had little hope, after what had occurred the other day in the Amescoas; and that the army under Valdés was insufficient. There were others, among whom San Miguel, the former Minister for Foreign Affairs under the Cortes in 1823, who strongly protested against French intervention, and who would not care if the whole of Navarre was ravaged, and army after army destroyed in carrying the devastation into effect—this merely for the humiliation which the nation, as well as the government, must necessarily undergo. I am not politician enough to guess even what other result may ensue from French intervention, but without it, it appears to me quite clear that this country must remain in eternal Civil War, if there should not be a worse consequence—the success of the Carlist cause, unfettered by any declaration of amnesty or guarantee. This would be worse even than Civil War, as the greater part of the nation, south of the Ebro, is compromised, and vengeance would reign with fanaticism. In this town the people have been in a state of siege for the last 14 months—there is a "Casa fuerte" here, with a small garrison, which keeps out the Carlists, although ninty-nine out of a hundred of the inhabitants, who cannot be less than 5000, are known to be Carlists. This is the case with every town in Navarre which we have seen or heard of. I told you in my last, that the last day I left Zumalacarregui's quarters at Asarta, on Tuesday last, the 28th, he was on the march— of course none but himself knew where; but the next day but one Valdés put his column in motion to follow the movement, supposed to be for the Bastan. You will easily see by the maps that by coming down to Viana, he has made two days useless march there, and two back— making four days very uselessly employed; for Zumalacarregui taking advantage of the no chance of interruption, directly proceeded to where the Christinos forces are least able to combat with his troops—and this day's rain has done Valdés' column more harm than half-a-dozen battles. Valdés is a very gentleman-like person in his manners—not so in appearance, for he looks like a "marchand de lorgnettes." He rides at the head of his column "en bourgeois," in a great green coat with sugar loaf buttons, and a plushy round hat, something in appearance between the "marchand de lorgnettes" and an American skipper! I very much doubt his having any professional talent; he does not know the value of soldiers, and the result of a march in such a cold watery day as this—for if he did, he could have put them up in the towns before they lost their shoes; and his object in endeavouring to overtake Zumalacarregui will not succeed. We shall see, however, in a few days. He marches his column to-morrow to Pamplona and its neighbourhood. We shall not start until the rain ceases.

Yours, &c,

(Signed) J. GURWOOD.

Pamplona, 3rd May.

My Dear Lord Fitzroy,

The weather cleared up and we came on here from Puente yesterday, passing the column on the road. The Infantry were in a most pitiable state from the heavy rain of the preceding day. It is said that Zumalacarregui had been attacking the fortified village of Irurzun, near the "Dos Hermanas," but had not succeeded; and on the appearance of Valdés' column on the hill from Puente, had desisted from farther attempts. We dined with Valdés, where we met Sancho, an officer who had been strongly recommended by Mina to the Government to be the chief of his staff, and said to be clever. He was very strong against a French armed intervention; stating that on the expiration of it, without it was intended to continue it for ever, Spain and the Queen's Government would be in a worse state than ever, and always subject to the insults of the two extreme parties that opposed the present order of things, which with time and good administration would certainly mature into strength. There were two other officers of the same opinions and who certainly argued well. It is evidently the feeling of the friends of Mina and of Mina himself. After dinner we went to the Palace, and were presented to General Mina and his wife by Colonel Wylde. Mina is evidently in bad health, and unequal to any active command. He appeared to have no doubt but that the Carlist faction could be shortly subdued by summary and energetic measures. This is all very well for him to say, but former experience has proved what Spanish "summary and energetic measures" are, to swagger and bully, burn some houses of defenceless inhabitants, and shoot half-a-dozen wretches who have been compromised by events which they could not avoid. The fact is, the more I see and the more I hear, the less I understand of what can be the results of this partisan warfare; for experience has proved that the present struggle, between the two armed forces, cannot be conducted upon any system known to the commanders of armies of civilised nations.

Nothing is more absurd and more annoying than the visits and compliments of the Spanish functionaries, and I should die no other death if obliged continually to undergo them. Our last dinner with Valdés to-day will, I hope, frank us till daylight, and night put us in St. Jean Pied de port.

Sincerely yours,

JOHN GURWOOD.

St. Jean Pied de port, Monday Night, 4 May.

PS.—We have arrived here, having been 14 hours on horseback, and we proceed to Bayonne to-morrow.

J. G.

APPENDIX.

Memorandum of my first conversation with His Royal Highness the Duke d'Angouleme, August 19th, 1823.

Gibraltar, August 30th, 1823.

On my arrival at Port St. Mary's, I went to the Duke d'Angouleme's head quarters, and was at once admitted into His Royal Highness's presence.

He received me courteously, and then proceeded to read the letter from you, which I delivered to him.

A long conversation ensued, in the course of which he spoke without reserve of his own position, saying that his hands were tied, and that he could take no step which the French Government had not specially authorised him to take. As a proof of this he showed me the draft of a letter which he had addressed to the King of Spain on the 19th inst. The draft had been sent to him from Paris, and he had not thought himself at liberty to make any, even verbal, alterations in it. No discretionary power whatever had in fact been vested in him.

He seemed to be desirous to learn what concessions the Cortes would, in your opinion, be now disposed to make; but he repeated more than once that he could listen to no proposition of which the King of Spain's liberation did not form a part. If the King were allowed to confer privately with him, His Majesty's real wishes would be ascertained. Now, he was quite in the dark with regard to them. I said that it was impossible for you to speak, with any confidence, of the nature and extent of the concessions that the Cortes may now be willing to make, but that you had no doubt that the Cortes would insist on the establishment of a Legislature, representing the people, as a condition sine qua non of any treaty.

He fully admitted the propriety of this condition, declaring that no one could be a warmer admirer of a representative Government than himself, and that he attributed the present prosperity of France to her existing institutions. He confessed, however, that he did not see in this country the elements of a good representative body. The bigotry and ignorance of one party, the turbulence and the democratic spirit of the other would, he feared, render Constitutional Monarchy an impracticable form of government. Gloomy, indeed, he said, did the prospects of Spain appear to him to be.

He proceeded: We are much more liberal than you give us credit for being. The conduct of the Regency at Madrid has caused me very great anxiety. To break at once with the powerful party, of which they are the head, would have been impolitic in the highest degree; I have therefore not ventured to oppose them, or even to express openly my disapproval of their measures, but I have endeavoured to restrain their zeal, and have sometimes succeeded in doing so.

His Royal Highness proceeded to assure me that he would not delay to bring to the knowledge of the Cabinet of the Tuileries the communication of which I was the bearer. He had however, he said, but little hope that they would accept the offer that His Majesty's Government had instructed you to make.

His Royal Highness's tone throughout was that of a man sensible of the evils of the existing state of things, and desirous to put an end to it.

He expressed great confidence in your judgment and ability, and said that if his wishes were consulted, you would be the channel of communication between the Government of His Most Catholic Majesty and that of the Cortes.

On the whole, my interview with His Royal Highness was, I think, satisfactory, although he did not give me a categorical answer.

(SIGNED) E. G. ELIOT.

The Right Hon. Sir W. a'Court, Bart., G.C.B.
    &c. &c. &c.

Memorandum of my second and third interviews with the Duke d'Angouleme, September 12th and 13th, 1823.

Gibraltar, Sept. 15th, 1823.

I Found the Duke at Chiclana, and was admitted without delay into his presence.

I had no sooner presented your letter and its enclosures to him than he addressed me. If, said His Royal Highness, these papers contain the offer of a mediation, or even a suggestion that negotiations shall take place on board an English ship of war, made neutral for the purpose, I must at once tell you that nothing of the kind is possible. The instructions that I have lately received are clear and precise. I must now insist on the immediate and unqualified liberation of the King, by which, I understand his being allowed to repair unconditionally to my head quarters.

This is not the language which I held when I saw you at Port St. Mary's, but I had not then received these instructions. I have since been forbidden to listen to any proposal to mediate or to intervene that may be made by any foreign Power.

General Alava has been with me twice. He told me the first time he came that his Government would probably soon make such a suggestion as that of which I have spoken.

He came again on the 7th of this month, and then, after confessing that the besieged could not hold out much longer, discussed with me the terms of capitulation. Before he left me he expressed a confident hope that he should be able to bring me on the following day the capitulation ready for signature.

He has not come again. I have heard that after his return to Cadiz, the violent party found out what was going on, and by dint of clamour deterred the Government from carrying their design into effect.

I cannot affirm that this story is true, but I believe it to be so. At any rate I am satisfied that General Alava did not intentionally deceive me. He had nothing to gain by deceiving me. Moreover, I feel sure that he is incapable of telling a lie.

We are now, he continued, more than ever convinced that it is only by force of arms that we can deliver the King and the Royal Family.

On my observing that the King and the Royal Family would be exposed to great danger if an attack were made on the city, His Royal Highness said that this danger was, in his opinion, slight, not to say chimerical.

The Duke de Guiche's interview with the King had not, His Royal Highness told me, been a private one, M. Valdés, and other members of the party to which M. Valdés belongs, having been present at it.

His Royal Highness then, after expressing his conviction that the existing state of things would soon be brought to an end, dismissed me.

The next morning I again, by His Royal Highness's desire, waited on him. He said that he had read with attention the papers I had brought, but that he had found nothing in them that would warrant him in deviating from the line which his instructions traced out for him.

He even desired me to alter the postscript to your note to M. Luyando, which I had added, according to the directions that you gave me, and instead of saying that " His Royal Highness did not think himself authorized to accede to Sir William a Court's proposal, without the consent of the Cabinet of the Tuileries, to say only, that "His Royal Highness declined to accede to the proposal."

This was, as nearly as I can recollect it, the substance of what His Royal Highness said to me in the course of the two interviews with him, to which I was admitted at Chiclana.

      (Signed) E. G. Eliot.

The Right Hon. Sir W. A. Court, Bart., G.C.B.
 &c. &c. &c.

Made in the USA
Middletown, DE
21 March 2021